THE
TRAIN
NOW DEPARTING

— ○ ○ ○ —

THE TRAIN
NOW DEPARTING

— o o o —

**Personal memories of the
last days of steam**

**With classic
photographs by**
Ivo Peters

BBC BOOKS

THIS BOOK IS DEDICATED TO
THE RAILWAY MEN & WOMEN OF GREAT BRITAIN

The authors would like to thank Dick Riley for the use of his photographs and for advice and help throughout the production of this book; David Cross and David Lockett for the use of their late fathers' photographic collections; Brian Hawkins, co-director of the television series on which this book is based; and the entire team at BBC Books, including editors Linda Mallory and Sarah Hoggett, designer Rachel Hardman and picture researchers Paul Dowswell and Gwenan Morgan. Particular thanks are due to Nina Shandloff, who compiled, edited and at every stage looked after her fanatical contributors. She has been the anchor to our flights of fancy, producing what we hope is a book that can be enjoyed by enthusiast and non-enthusiast alike. And, of course, we would like to thank Ivo Peters, without whom neither this book nor the television series would have been possible.

The authors and publishers would also like to acknowledge permission to quote from Mike Arlett's article, 'Summer Saturdays at Swanage in the 1950s' (first published in *Steam Railway*, October 1986); from Bill Peacock's article, 'Main Line to Hawick' (Cheviot Publications, Hawick, Roxburghshire); and from Ivo Peters' previously published account of his visit to the Isle of Man.

Published by BBC Books
A division of BBC Enterprises Ltd
Woodlands, 80 Wood Lane
London W12 OTT

First published 1988

Text © Mike Arlett, Peter Handford, Andrew Johnston,
David Rowlands, Eric Tonks and David Wilcock 1988

ISBN 0 563 20696 9

Typeset in 11 on 14 point Imprint and printed and bound
in England by Butler & Tanner Ltd, Frome and London
Colour printed by Chorley & Pickersgill Ltd, Leeds
Jacket printed by Belmont Press Ltd

CONTENTS

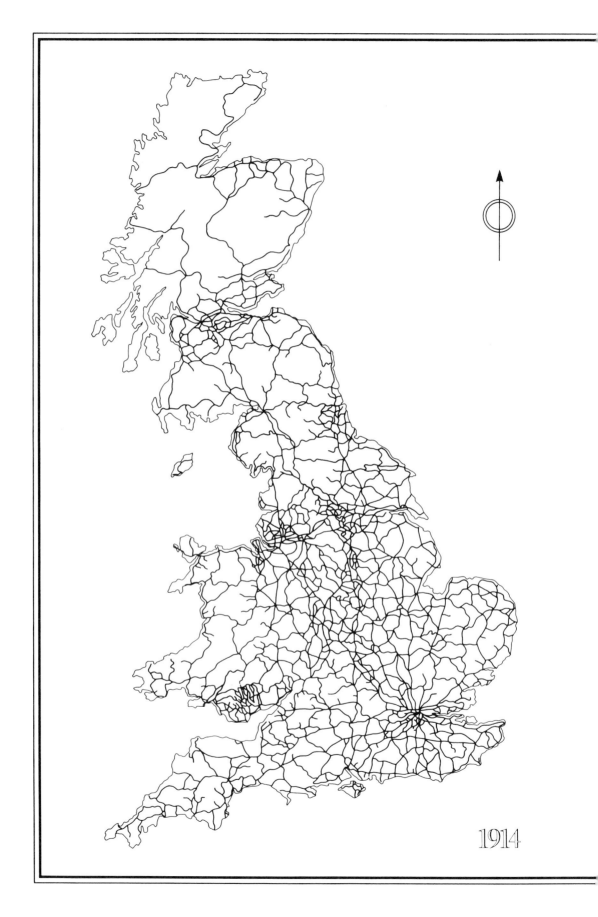

1914

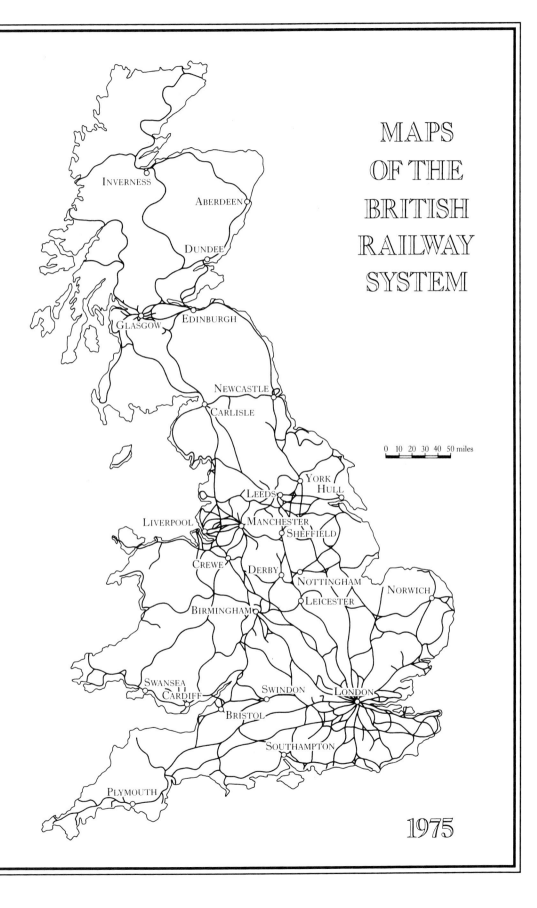

MAPS
OF THE
BRITISH
RAILWAY
SYSTEM

0 10 20 30 40 50 miles

INVERNESS

ABERDEEN

DUNDEE

GLASGOW   EDINBURGH

NEWCASTLE

CARLISLE

YORK
HULL

LEEDS

LIVERPOOL   MANCHESTER
SHEFFIELD

CREWE   DERBY
NOTTINGHAM
NORWICH
LEICESTER

BIRMINGHAM

SWANSEA
CARDIFF   SWINDON   LONDON

BRISTOL

SOUTHAMPTON

PLYMOUTH

1975

Preserved Stanier class 5 No. 5305 at Blea Moor tunnel, 8 March 1986.

STEAM
IN THE HILLS

DAVID WILCOCK

Back in the early-to-mid 1960s, The Junction Hotel at Tebay was notable for the fact that it served quite the most appalling pint of bitter anywhere in Westmorland. Whatever it was that Dutton's of Blackburn put into their foul, watery brew, it tasted absolutely awful. Anyone who stayed at The Junction around that time certainly wasn't there for the beer.

At twenty-five bob (£1.25) a night for bed and breakfast, it was cheap – but it was also a dingy, down-at-heel place, with faded wallpaper in the bedrooms, worn carpets on the stairs and landing, and that slightly musty smell that one associates with under-ventilated old buildings. Cold and uninviting, it was the classic 'commercial' hotel, totally lacking in character. Anyone who stayed at The Junction certainly wasn't there for the atmosphere either.

But for the steady stream of railway enthusiasts who stopped there – and who kept coming back – The Junction was the perfect place to be, for several good reasons. It was immediately adjacent to Tebay station, and since most railway buffs arrived at Tebay by train, it had all the virtues of convenience. It was probably the only hotel in the world to offer darkroom and film-processing facilities to its railway enthusiast guests, highlighting the fact with an advertisement in the classified columns of *Trains Illustrated* magazine. But most important of all was its strategic location. Situated some 700 ft up in the Westmorland fells, it marked the start of the most arduous railway gradient anywhere in England – the 4 miles of 1 in 75 known as Shap.

True, there were more severe climbs on other lines – the 'mountain' which Southern Railway locomotives had to conquer on their way out of Ilfracombe was more than twice as steep at 1 in 36 – but it was only half the distance, and even express trains were restricted to just three coaches, unless a second engine was put on to share the load.

Shap was different. It was the place where the London–Glasgow main line finally confronted the high Pennines, some 262 miles north of Euston's wooden platforms. The place where a driver's skill and a fireman's stamina were tested to the full on heavy express passenger trains of 15, 16 and 17 coaches. The place where railway enthusiasts in their scores came to see the ultimate test of steam power, amid the dramatic and beautiful limestone country.

The Junction Hotel, however, was not alone in making overtures to railway enthusiasts. In those same classified columns, another advertisement persuaded the disciples of steam to 'enjoy loco performance over Shap from the comforts of our farm situated near Scout Green signal box. Rooms afford

ABOVE *On a cold April morning in 1966, Stanier class 5 No. 45449 grinds up the Fell to Shap with rear-end assistance from the banking engine.*

RIGHT *Coming down was easy! Here a Stanier class 5 drifts through the Lune Gorge with a long southbound train of empty wagons.*

excellent views of line. Bed, breakfast and evening meal 22s. 6d. Apply: Mrs Thackeray, High Scales, Shap, Penrith, Cumberland.'

Agnes Thackeray's place was a 2-mile walk from Tebay station and it didn't have the darkroom facilities; but amidst a homely, cosy atmosphere, there was traditional farmhouse cooking, home-made bread and tea-cakes, and the welcome of an open fire on chilly evenings. When, around 1965, the message really struck home that steam was on a very short fuse, railway buffs came to Shap in waves, equipped with cameras, notebooks, tape recorders and cine cameras, to record the last blood-stirring moments, and it was not uncommon for all nine beds at High Scales to be taken.

For others, simple economics dictated a canvas roof, and never mind the midge bites. When the mist settled in on the fells late on a Friday afternoon, there wasn't a tent to be seen; but by the time the mist lifted the following morning, as many as half a dozen tents might have sprouted on the damp grass, pitched in the shelter of the dry stone walls either side of the line by Scout Green box, or down amongst the rocky Birk Beck, which ran parallel to the line.

The all-night percussion of freight trains slogging up the 1 in 75, usually with a banking engine from Tebay shed at the rear, or the more urgent rasp of the overnight sleeping-car expresses on their 401-mile trek from Euston to Glasgow Central, was stereophonic music to fill the ears – and what better sound was there for a devoted steam enthusiast to go to sleep to, or, indeed, be awoken by?

Shap in steam days was one of Britain's great railway legends, but enthusiast ecstasies about men and machines performing heroic deeds in the face of the Pennine challenge, with heavy, 500-ton-plus trains, meant little to the railway companies who had to get on with the business of operating trains on the route. To British Railways and its predecessors the London, Midland & Scottish Railway, the London & North Western Railway, and the Lancaster & Carlisle Railway, Shap was more realistically an impediment which required special arrangements to ease the path for trains going north to Carlisle and Glasgow.

Shap could have been rather less of an operating burden if, instead of climbing over the fells, the line had been driven through them, via a deep tunnel, and in fact when a railway over the west Pennines was first considered back in the 1840s, such a proposal was put forward. But the 4 miles of 1 in 75 really became inescapable when, at a public meeting in Carlisle in 1841, Captain Mark Huish of the Grand Junction Railway, one of three companies promoting the new line, emphasised: 'The projectors of the line must above all things consider economy. They must be satisfied to go over the hills, not through them ... the question of gradients is daily assuming less importance.'

His words had some truth, although it was not until 1974, when electrification to Glasgow was finally completed, that advanced technology finally 'flattened' the gradients of Shap.

The first passenger train over Shap, a nine-coach special carrying some 200 passengers, ran on the icy afternoon of 15 December 1846, to mark the opening of the 70-mile line between Lancaster and Carlisle. Hauled by a spartan, cabless engine called *Dalemain*, designed by Richard Trevithick and Alexander Allan and sporting a massive single pair of driving wheels, it took the bank at a steady $22\frac{1}{2}$ mph without assistance – a creditable performance.

That same week, the building contractor John Stephenson predicted that improved locomotive designs would make 30 mph possible on the bank 'or even twice that speed' – but it was another 90 years before his second forecast was fulfilled.

The average speed of $64\frac{1}{2}$ mph maintained between Tebay and Shap

Summit on 16 November 1936, by the now preserved L M S 'Princess' loco-motive No. 6201 *Princess Elizabeth*, with the pace never dropping below 57 mph, still stands today as one of steam's best-ever performances on the climb, even though the load was a modest 230 tons.

More usually, the heavy expresses hauled by L M S 'Duchess' and 'Princess' class Pacifics raced through Tebay at around 60 mph, and were down to the 20s by the time they were going over the summit 4 miles later. The great billowing exhausts and staccato beat which echoed back from the bleak moor-land in between times was what the magnetism of Shap was all about – and, if the sun shone, there was no finer place in England for a railway enthusiast to be. Unfortunately, the weather in the fells was often every bit as foul as Dutton's bitter.... which conveniently brings us back to The Junction Hotel.

The fact that The Junction was conveniently located just one minute's walk from Tebay station also meant that the hotel came well within the sootfall of Tebay engine shed. During the 1950s and 1960s, Tebay shed maintained an allocation of around 10 steam locomotives, at least half of which were 2–6–4 tank engines, of L M S origin. Their prime function, and indeed the principal reason why Tebay had a loco depot in the first place, was to provide banking assistance – in simple language, a helping shove from the back – for the heavier trains tackling Shap from the south.

The general rule was that the drivers of all goods trains exceeding 19 wagons plus guard's brake van, and those of other trains which needed a banker, would sound three blasts or 'crows' on the whistle as they approached Tebay No. 1 signal box through the Lune Gorge. That was the cue to the crew of the loco on banking duty that their services were required. As soon as the Carlisle-bound train had passed, the points would be switched across for the banker to slip out of its siding, close the gap on the last coach or wagon of the train, and, touching buffer-to-buffer, keep pushing until the train had cleared Shap Summit signal box and begun its downhill run towards Penrith and the border. Then the banker would cross on to the 'Up' (London-bound) line, and set off back to the shed, there to await the next call for help.

At least, that was the theory. In practice, it was not unknown for the crew of an advancing heavy freight or passenger train to whistle the 'banker needed' call sign – and then go hell-for-leather for the summit, with the aim of shaking off the pursuing tank engine before it had the chance to buffer-up. There were many instances of banking engines going all the way to the summit without ever making contact with the train they were supposed to be assisting. Such 'humour' was not always appreciated by the Tebay men.

Right from the very early days of the Lancaster & Carlisle Railway, Tebay had kept a banking engine to help trains up the 4 miles of 1 in 75; but the London & North Western Railway, which took over the Shap route in 1879, had other ideas. For a period around the turn of the century, the banking of express passenger trains was abandoned in favour of double-heading – the practice of coupling two engines together at the front of trains, from Crewe through to Carlisle.

While Shap was definitely the serious bit for enginemen, it was regarded by many as being no more than the final hard slog at the end of a climb which really began 19 miles south of Tebay, at the foot of Grayrigg bank. Grayrigg, although a 13-mile climb, was nowhere near as severe as Shap, and, once over the summit, enginemen had the respite of $5\frac{1}{2}$ miles of level or downhill running through the beautiful Lune Gorge, during which time steam could be shut off, and a fireman had the opportunity to rebuild his fire, and so give the engine 'second wind' for the assault on Shap itself.

However, midway up Grayrigg bank came Oxenholme, the junction station for Kendal and the Windermere branch, and those trains obliged to make a stop there had to restart on a rising gradient of 1 in 178 – no simple task for the heavier trains, especially on wet rails.

ABOVE *2–6–4 tank No. 42251 running back to Oxenholme for its next banking duty.*
TOP RIGHT *Stanier class 5 No. 44672 passes Grayrigg box with a heavy parcels train. The black exhaust is evidence of hard work with the fireman's shovel.*

So Oxenholme, like Tebay, kept banking engines at the ready for those trains which needed them. About eight L M S tank engines were allocated to the small engine shed there, both for banking duties and work on the Windermere branch, and even when Oxenholme shed closed in 1962, banking continued, with engines sent 'down the hill' from Tebay.

The distance from the foot of Grayrigg bank to the summit of Shap was a little under 25 miles, and when steam ruled the West Coast rails, train movements over that stretch were regulated by no fewer than 15 signal boxes, the number being decided not only by the presence of junctions at Hincaster, Oxenholme, Lowgill and Tebay, but also by the need to divert slow trains into the 'loops' on the climb, out of the path of fast-running expresses like the non-stop 'Royal Scot'.

Traditionally, signal boxes had notices bolted to their doors, proclaiming: 'No admittance, except on official business'. But, with a few exceptions, the men who kept the trains running over Shap and Grayrigg gave a sympathetic welcome to unofficial visitors. Many were the enthusiasts and photographers who discovered the sweet, syrupy taste of 'signal-box tea' while watching trains toil over the high northern fells.

Scout Green, the modest little signal cabin halfway up Shap bank, boasted

A class 5 hammers past Scout Green signal box in April 1965.

just seven levers and a set of crossing gates over a minor road to Penrith, but it was without doubt the best-known and most frequently visited box anywhere on the climb. It was easily distinguished from all others by its chimney stack, which perpetually leaned at 25 degrees to the perpendicular, and by the massively tall semaphore signal which towered above it.

The Shap line, being one of the two main rail arteries between London and Scotland, and with branches off to Birmingham, Liverpool and Manchester, has never known the threat of closure – but the character of the line has almost ebbed away since the last days of steam, in the summer of 1968. Electric trains, drawing all the power they need from the National Grid, flash up the 1 in 75 as if it isn't there. The concept of man and machine battling against adverse terrain and elements is just so much history.

Agnes Thackeray, still hale and hearty at 84 but no longer in the bed, breakfast and evening meal business, looks out across the misty fells to the spot where Scout Green box and its tall signal used to stand, and remembers how, in the days before they truncated the road and closed the crossing, she would pause briefly to exchange the time of day with signalmen Tommy Satterthwaite, Joe Murray and Hughie Bernard.

Down in Tebay, retired signalman Joe Murray recalls how the railway enthusiasts used to 'trail up and down the railway side all night, looking for places to put up their tents' – in the days before he worked the very last shift in Scout Green box, on 15 April 1973.

High on the fellsides, the M6 motorway now follows the line from Grayrigg, through the Lune Gorge to Tebay, passing on its way the level stretch at Dillicar where water troughs between the rails allowed steam locomotive crews to scoop water into their tenders without slowing down as they raced towards Shap.

Across the valley, the rows of railway cottages built by the London & North Western Railway and the North Eastern Railway back in the 1860s gaze down on only the recollection of a station and an engine shed, both of which died with the age of steam in 1968.

And The Junction? The railway buffs who stopped there 25 years ago and more would hardly recognise today's rather more up-market Lune Valley Hotel as the seedy place which served up Dutton's bitter to unsuspecting victims. The brewery, I am reliably informed, closed down over a decade ago.

Well, at least some things have changed for the better.

TOP LEFT *9F No. 92019 picks up water on Dillicar Troughs while running south in the Lune Gorge, in July 1966.*

LEFT *There are few reasons now to pitch a tent at Shap Wells and wait for the next goods train to climb the bank.*

ABOVE *Once the peace of the Lune Gorge was disturbed only by the passing of trains. Now it is also pounded by the constant roar of the M6 traffic. In the summer of 1966, 'Britannia' Pacific No. 70013 'Oliver Cromwell' heads south with empty wagons.*

In the pitch blackness of Blea Moor, beneath the towering Pennine rampart known as Whernside, the dim glow of a gas lamp pinpoints the only sign of life for miles around. It is Blea Moor signal box, and of all the wild and inhospitable places in England anyone could choose to put a signal box, Blea Moor is perhaps the wildest and least hospitable of them all.

Over a mile from the nearest road and approached on foot via a narrow path through the peat bogs of Blea Moor itself, it could scarcely be more exposed to the fierce winds which gust around it at 60 mph. Water is delivered in canisters by passing trains; electricity is something that belongs to civilisation.

Since just before 10.00p.m. when he booked on duty, signalman George Horner has been kept busy by the procession of night freights banging and jostling their noisy way between Leeds and Carlisle, and now, as the hands of the clock move round towards 1.30a.m., an unusual lull descends on the line.

Filling the kettle and placing it on the stove, he settles down into the signalman's chair to read what is now yesterday's paper. The rhythmic ticking of the clock and the gentle hiss of the gas burner on the stove are the only sounds to be heard in the sanctuary of Blea Moor box.

ABOVE *Signalman George Horner returns to his old box at Blea Moor for filming the television series 'The Train Now Departing'.*

RIGHT *Preserved Stanier Pacific 'Duchess of Hamilton' blackens the sky as it passes the lonely Blea Moor signal box with a steam special on the Settle–Carlisle line.*

Suddenly, urgently, the telephone rings. The light on the instrument shelf shows that the call is coming from a lineside telephone only a quarter of a mile away, out in the darkness at the south end of Blea Moor loops.

Who on earth could be ringing from a telephone in the middle of the moor at this time of night? And more importantly, perhaps, why? It is nearly eight hours since the track gang finished work.

Cautiously, he picks up the receiver.

'Hello?'

For a moment there is nothing.

'Hello?'

Then the breathing starts. Long, slow, asthmatic gasps, becoming progressively louder.

'Hello? Who is this? Hello?'

A chill air seems to circulate in Blea Moor box, causing the hairs on the back of the neck to bristle. Signalman Horner jams the receiver down sharply, and strides down the length of the box, to lock the door from the inside.

The phone didn't ring again that night.

It was George Horner himself who told me this story several years ago, and although signalmen's yarns can sometimes be more broadly spun that fishermen's tales, there was something in George Horner's eyes that told me this was no fiction.

The story conveys the remoteness, not just of Blea Moor, but of the Settle & Carlisle railway as a whole – geographically, historically and strategically. But you'd need to have had your head in a bucket of sand these past few years not to have heard of the line. It has been the subject of three House of Commons debates, three TUCC (Transport Users' Consultative Committee) inquiries, numerous television documentaries and investigations, newspaper coverage which runs into column miles rather than column inches – and the most professional, aggressive and organised anti-closure campaign ever mounted in defence of a British railway.

Never before has a railway enjoyed such universal or passionate public support. Never before has any railway inspired the creation of a limited company (with its own permanent offices) to defend its future. Never before has so much money – nearly £2 million – been pledged by private, public and independent organisations to develop a line. But in May 1988, the Government turned its back on all the arguments, condemning the Settle & Carlisle to closure by Easter 1989 unless a private buyer is found – and of that, the Government itself knows, there is little prospect.

As far back as 1963, the Settle & Carlisle was on the hit list drawn up by Dr Beeching in his *Reshaping of British Railways*, the blueprint for a holocaust. But the line was then still regarded as an important trunk route, and it survived and outlived him.

But we're racing ahead; before looking at how and why British Rail decided to pursue closure of the Midland Railway's superbly scenic Pennine route, we should look at how and why it was created in the first place. It is sometimes said that the Settle & Carlisle was a line that should never have been built, and but for the bloody-mindedness of the rival London & North Western Railway, it never would have been.

TOP RIGHT *Leaving Blea Moor, 9F No. 92019 heads south towards Ribblehead with the regular anhydrite (plaster of Paris) train to Widnes.*

Back in the 1860s, the Midland Railway had extended its operations to Bristol in the west, and as far north as north Yorkshire – but it had no route of its own into Scotland. What the Midland did have was an agreement with the L&NWR, to hand over all its Scottish-bound traffic at Ingleton, from where the L&NWR would carry it forward via Low Gill and the Shap route, to Carlisle.

In practice, the L&NWR came to give only its own passengers and goods any priority; for the Midland's traffic there was a distinct lack of enthusiasm. By 1866, the Midland Railway had secured Parliamentary consent to drive its own line to Carlisle, and in spite of a rather late capitulation by the London & North Western and even a willingness to co-operate by the Midland, an Abandonment Bill failed to get through Parliament. The Midland had no choice but to go ahead with its new line.

The way north was formidable, for wherever the Midland decided to start its line, it couldn't escape the great limestone hills and deep valleys that made up the backbone of the high Pennines; and neither could it ignore the fact that the weather at such altitudes, particularly in winter, could be quite brutal.

That fact wasn't lost on C. S. Sharland, the young engineer sent to plot the course of the new line; for a three-week spell during the survey, he was totally snowbound in the wayside inn at Gearstones, near Ribblehead.

It was clear that for a railway to traverse such terrain would demand engineering on a scale never attempted before, and while the $72\frac{1}{2}$-mile route chosen by Sharland followed the natural course of the River Ribble from Settle to Blea Moor, and the River Eden from Culgaith almost to Carlisle, the section in between required at least a dozen viaducts and five major tunnels – the longest of which, Blea Moor, would be $1\frac{1}{2}$ miles long, and hewn out of solid limestone up to 500 feet below ground level.

The completed line which opened for freight traffic in August 1875 actually included 14 tunnels, an abundance of 'edge of a ledge' running, and 19 major viaducts, including the legendary quarter-mile 24-span Ribblehead Viaduct. No appraisal of the s & c would be complete without some mention of the engineering skill and commitment that resulted in the completion of this magnificent monolith.

ABOVE *Ribblehead Viaduct under construction in the early 1870s.*

TOP RIGHT *Ribblehead in the 1960s, with 'Britannia' Pacific No. 70010 'Owen Glendower' heading north to Blea Moor.*

The statistics are that Ribblehead Viaduct was built over a five-year period, from limestone quarried beside the route of the line between Selside and Ribblehead itself. Begun in 1870, its piers are sunk 25 feet below moor level and rise 165 feet above it.

Simple statistics, however, do not reveal that thousands of railway navvies, billeted in hutted encampments around Ribblehead and Blea Moor, lived and died for the building of the viaduct. Irish, Scots, Cornishmen and Lancastrians came with their families, fought bloody battles with one another, stole, swore, survived a smallpox epidemic, and even fell to their deaths from the 'scaffolding' during those pioneering days of the Victorian era.

The Settle & Carlisle left the Midland Railway with little change from £3½ million, or £47 500 a mile. But for the availability of dynamite – then a quite new aid to railway construction – the costs would have been much greater.

The S&C was the Midland's crowning glory in terms of engineering achievement – but, 110 years later, the cost of maintaining those magnificent viaducts and tunnels was to threaten the very existence of the route. The line began in London at St Pancras, and followed a route through Bedford, Wellingborough, Leicester, Nottingham, Sheffield and Leeds – but then over the next 112 miles to Carlisle it served no major centre of population at all. While that did the S&C no favours, particularly in more recent times when the usefulness of the route was called into question, the fact remains that it was – and still is – the quickest and most direct rail route from the Midlands and the Leeds area to Scotland.

Under the control of the London, Midland & Scottish Railway for 25 years from 1923, the S&C changed little, and initially, under the BR regime begun in 1948, it seemed quite secure. At one stage, it was viewed by Robert Riddles, design chief on the new Railway Executive, as the candidate for a pilot electrification scheme, but, in the event, a very much less adventurous programme was adopted on the Lancaster–Morecambe–Heysham route.

The Settle & Carlisle was to be BR's last steam-worked main line, and although the final train – the now legendary '15 Guinea Special' – on 11 August

ABOVE *Stanier class 5 Nos. 44871 and 44781 at Ribblehead with British Rail's very last steam train on 11 August 1968.*

RIGHT *Aisgill signal box, with 9F No. 92110 about to begin the downhill run to Settle.*

1968 brought quite unbelievable traffic jams to the normally quiet B6259 road over Aisgill summit, the fact was that many enthusiasts were seeing the Settle & Carlisle for only the first time.

Shap was usually the preferred option for most steam buffs, for it boasted the more famous trains, like the 'Royal Scot' and 'The Caledonian', and, in the LMS 'Duchess' and 'Princess' Pacifics, the most worshipped locomotives of any then running on BR metals.

On the S&C, both the LMS and British Railways had more or less followed the Midland Railway practice of running smaller or less powerful engines on its expresses, resorting to double-heading on trains like 'The Thames–Clyde Express' (St Pancras–Glasgow St Enoch) when the need arose. And, although the S&C was infinitely more dramatic in its Pennine scenery and architecture, Scout Green would beat Aisgill in a tent-count on most weekends.

There were, however, some interesting similarities and comparisons to be made between the Shap and Aisgill lines. For all Shap's intensity, Aisgill, at 1169 feet above sea level, was – and still is – England's highest rail way summit, having inherited that status when the Kirkby Stephen–Darlington route over Stainmore summit (1370 feet) was axed by BR in 1962.

To the steam firemen of Leeds, Skipton, Hellifield and Carlisle engine sheds, whose job it was to get heavy (and sometimes impossibly heavy) trains over that Pennine hump, 'feet above sea level' was of academic interest only. The reality was that a man could be shovelling coal non-stop for 40 minutes,

just to keep up steam on those grinding, back-breaking approaches to Aisgill, shifting perhaps $\frac{3}{4}$ ton of coal in the process. The Settle & Carlisle was a hard railway for a young fireman; only after the summit was passed could he stop to wring out his shirt, and take in some of the magnificent mountain scenery.

Whether taking on the unrelenting 15 miles of 1 in 100 from Settle Junction to Blea Moor (the stretch dubbed 'the Long Drag' by enginemen, for obvious reasons), or tackling the similarly graded 16-mile northern slope from Ormside to Aisgill itself, a footplateman's credibility and reputation was on the line, every time. There was always the stigma of defeat if ever a crew had to 'stop for a blow-up' (remake the fire to resuscitate falling steam pressure), even though this often had more to do with the condition of the engine or quality of the coal than the competence of the men on the footplate.

ABOVE *Stanier class 8F No. 48421 in the Mallerstang Valley nearing the end of the climb to Aisgill with a southbound train of soda ash.*

RIGHT *9F No. 92071 passing Kirkby Stephen signal box and its towering home signal.*

The S&C never had a busy local passenger service, even though the Midland Railway built no fewer than 18 stations along its $72\frac{1}{2}$-mile route. The 1953 service of four stopping trains in the down (northbound) direction and five in the up, reflected the fact that most of the communities served by the railway were farming ones, while a preponderance of sheep and cattle pens at almost every station testified that the S&C's best customers were four-legged.

Still, that was of small consequence; the key role of the S&C always was as a through route to Carlisle and Scotland, both for long-distance passengers and for freight. So Beeching's proposals to withdraw *all* passenger services from the line came as a real bombshell. In fact the S&C eluded Beeching altogether, and it wasn't until May 1970 – two years after the steam finale on the Settle & Carlisle – that the local passenger service was withdrawn, and 12 of the surviving 14 stations: Horton-in-Ribblesdale, Ribblehead, Dent, Garsdale, Kirkby Stephen, Long Marton, Newbiggin, Culgaith, Langwathby, Little Salkeld, Lazonby and Armathwaite – were closed.

That left the remaining stations at Settle and Appleby with just three trains a day in each direction – almost the bare minimum necessary for BR to

honour its statutory obligation to maintain a service. Subsequently, in May 1982, BR stripped the S&C of its 'InterCity' status, diverting the six Nottingham–Glasgow expresses to run via the much longer West Coast Main Line route to Carlisle. The reason, it was claimed, was 'to more effectively utilise the railway's resources'.

In their place, a Leeds–Carlisle 'local' service of four trains was introduced – but timed so as to miss vital connections to the south. The first train into Leeds didn't arrive until 12.48p.m., missing a connecting train to King's Cross by three minutes, and a Sheffield–Birmingham–South Wales connection by 14 minutes.

Anyone who witnessed the rundown of provincial railways in the 1960s – the Bath–Bournemouth Somerset & Dorset line comes to mind as an obvious example – would recognise the classic British Rail ploy of deliberately making the train service so ineffective as to drive passengers away, thus reinforcing the argument for closure with the claim that the railway is little used.

Whenever confronted by the accusation that BR was seeking to close the Settle & Carlisle by stealth, the Board's publicity officers clung to the claim that 'no decision has yet been reached' – a phrase which, in the light of a later discovery, was unlikely ever to be believed again. The official line was that the S&C had the status of a diversionary route.

Another element of the farce was revealed in the April 1981 issue of *Steam World* magazine, when BR divisional civil engineer Alan King claimed that Ribblehead Viaduct, the magnificent 24-arch structure taking the line across the neck of Chapel-le-Dale, was crumbling away. 'Three years might see it through,' he said, 'five years or thereabouts would be the limit.' BR's reasons for closure, it seemed, had gained a new dimension: the possibility of structural failure. A replacement viaduct, it was claimed, would cost £6 million or more (a figure which, in the face of public calls for an independent survey, was later to be revised downwards on several occasions). But, said BR, 'it would be difficult to justify expenditure of such a magnitude'.

In August 1983, after first arranging the diversion of Settle & Carlisle freight trains to other, more circuitous routes, BR finally came clean and announced it was seeking closure of the line. But a leaked copy of the minutes of a Railway Executive Group meeting confirmed what many people had suspected: that the decision to pursue closure of the Settle & Carlisle line had in fact been taken three years earlier.

BR public image was further discredited when the Settle–Carlisle Joint Action Committee (the group established to co-ordinate the fight against

closure) discovered that B R had contributed to the worsening state of Ribblehead Viaduct by neglecting to seal up its surface decking after drilling bore-
holes into the piers, in the early 1970s, in order to examine the state of the
mortar inside them. The unprotected piers had absorbed all the rain the
Pennine weather could throw at them, and over 15 or 16 winters, sub-zero
temperatures had caused the trapped rainwater to freeze, with consequent –
and inevitable – cracking of the main limestone structure.

But Ribblehead was only part of the problem. In July 1984 when an
Edinburgh firm of transport consultants delivered their independent report
on the line (conducted for Cumbria and West Yorkshire County Councils),
they found B R guilty of 'wanton neglect' on a grand scale.

Publicly lambasted for the bungling which led to the formal closure
notices having to be published on no less than three occasions, B R, after five
years of unprecedented public pressure, gave in to demands for a revitalised
train service on this immensely popular Pennine route. The summer service
operated in 1988 – five stopping passenger trains a day in each direction – was
as good as anything the Midland Railway ever envisaged, while the re-opening
of the s & c's closed stations in July 1986, and subsequent 'adoption' of them
by groups or individuals, was a move quite unparalleled in railway history.

In looking for reasons for the Settle & Carlisle line's remarkable popularity,
it is impossible to dismiss the return of steam-hauled excursions to the route in
1978. Where once ran 'The Thames–Clyde Express' now came the 'Cumbrian
Mountain Express' enthusiasts' specials, and, in more recent times, the more
up-market £55-a-head 'Pennine Limited' dining-car trains, hauled beneath
the towering peaks of Pen-y-Ghent, Ingleborough and Whernside by some of
the very locomotives that were banished from the line in B R's brave new world
of dieselisation in the 1960s.

Now magnificently restored and in private ownership, the L M S 'Black 5s'
and 'Jubilees', which carried the Settle & Carlisle reputation in steam days,
have over the past decade played a significant role in introducing the line to
those who previously knew nothing of it – although these days *two* firemen are
considered necessary to share the work up 'the Long Drag'. Highlighting
the outstanding scenic, recreational and architectural value of the route, the
modern-day steam excursions have spawned a huge following.

Only a handful of railway enthusiasts saw the last wheezing, grime-
encrusted days of steam on the s & c in the 1960s; today they arrive in carloads,

and by the hundreds, when engines like the LMS 'Pacific' No. 46229 *Duchess of Hamilton* are sounding the echoes up the Ribble Valley, or down beside the fertile pastures of the River Eden. A simultaneous growth in local tourism and outdoor pursuits such as hiking and fell-walking, and the willingness of local people to use the trains when BR provides a useful service (as distinct from a token one), have boosted passenger receipts and given a nationwide base to the S&C's popularity.

ABOVE *Preserved Stanier class 5 No. 5305 on an enthusiast special, March 1986.*

TOP RIGHT *The possible closure of a line as scenic as the Settle–Carlisle is seen by many as a return to the dark days of Dr Beeching.*

The anti-closure campaign, brilliantly co-ordinated by the Settle–Carlisle Joint Action Committee, resulted in formal objections being lodged by no fewer than 22 500 people – a quite unprecedented figure. And although BR continued to pursue its ill-conceived goal on financial grounds, the offer of nearly £2 million in grants and subsidies by English Heritage, Cumbria, Lancashire and North Yorkshire County Councils and private sector backers led S&C supporters to believe that, at last, the pendulum was swinging in their favour.

Then, on 16 May 1988, came the devastating news, delivered by Transport Minister David Mitchell, that the Government 'was minded to allow the closure', and he added: 'BR's priority is to invest in a modern rail system for the twenty-first century, not provide pleasure rides for railway archaeologists'.

The verdict was met with disbelief almost everywhere. At Appleby, a children's party at the railway station, arranged to celebrate the saving of the line, was called off. The Chairman of the Settle–Carlisle Joint Action Committee, Peter Horton, asserted, 'The Government just didn't listen. It's like Beeching all over again.' By the time these words go into print, the Settle & Carlisle will either be rejoicing in an eleventh-hour reprieve, brought about by sheer weight of public outcry, or becoming reconciled to the likelihood that come Easter 1989, the demolition gangs will move in to rip up the lines upon which has grown a legend. May God forgive the politicians, for there are many people who never will.

In 1967, the last year of Southern steam, 'Battle of Britain' class Pacific No. 34077 '603 Squadron', already stripped of its nameplates, stands in Nine Elms Depot.

SOUTH WESTERN
MEMORIES

—◦2◦—

MIKE ARLETT

The era of the L&SWR – the London & South Western Railway Company – came to an end some two decades before I was born. In 1923, the L&SWR, affectionately remembered as the old 'South Western', became a part of the newly formed Southern Railway when, in that year, the many independent railways of the British Isles were consolidated into just four major companies – the Great Western, the Southern, the London Midland & Scottish, and the London & North Eastern.

Just twenty-five years later, these companies, in turn, ceased to exist when, in 1948, the railways of Britain were nationalised to become British Railways. Yet even today, after the passage of a further forty years, there are still to be found reminders not only of the Southern Railway, but of the London & South Western. Around 1950, when as a small boy I first became interested in railways, there were still numerous examples of locomotives and rolling stock, of buildings, signals and other artefacts, all of which dated back to London & South Western days. True, the livery of the old company had long since disappeared under the hue of Southern Railway green, which in turn saw yet further changes following nationalisation, but at many a country station, there was little to indicate any of these changes in ownership.

My first encounter with the former L&SW system must have taken place at Salisbury in about 1950 or 1951. My father was fond of arranging family visits to cathedrals, churches and the like, but I quickly became bored, and

27

begged to be let off at the nearest station, where I could spend a happy few hours while my parents pursued their interests. And so, accompanying my parents on a visit to Salisbury, I was set down in Fisherton Street, and for the next two or three hours, was free to explore Salisbury station.

Having purchased for a penny a platform ticket, the initial task was to walk the full length of each platform and establish the best location for 'locospotting'. Until the mid-1960s, Salisbury station formed a busy railway crossroads, located about mid-distance between London and Exeter on the main line from Waterloo to the West Country, and intersected by the important cross-country route from south Wales and Bristol to Southampton, Portsmouth and Brighton. Other lines branched away from the Southampton route, to run to Eastleigh, and via Ringwood and Wimborne to Poole and Bournemouth. All of these lines, with the exception of that from Bristol, had once formed part of the L&SWR system. The line from Bristol was of GWR origin, and for many years terminated at a separate station in Salisbury, immediately to the north of the present station, which had been rebuilt by the L&SWR to accept Great Western traffic in 1902.

ABOVE *S15 class No. 30835 waits for signals at Salisbury station in March 1964.*
RIGHT *Two unrebuilt Bulleid Light Pacifics stand face to face on Salisbury shed.*

I soon found that platform 6, which extended some distance beyond the rest of the station, provided the ideal position for the enthusiast to observe the heavy express trains pulling away as they recommenced their journey towards London. A walk to the end of platform 6 also revealed a mysterious single track which turned away sharply and descended down a steep gradient to be lost from view. This was the Salisbury Market House Railway, a small and independent concern which had managed to escape nationalisation, and remained in private ownership. Perhaps this had something to do with the fact that the branch line was little more than a quarter of a mile in length! As the name suggests, it was originally promoted by local businessmen to connect the market with the main line. In later years, when serving only some warehouses, it was quite a rare event to see the local shunting engine heading off down the little line and later struggling back up the gradient with a rake of wagons.

I cannot pretend to recall much of my first visit to Salisbury station. One feature I still remember vividly, however, was my first sight of a Southern Railway Bulleid Light Pacific, a class of locomotive which was to remain my personal favourite. What so fascinated me about this particular class of railway engine was its appearance – quite unlike anything I had seen previously. There was no sign of the traditional cylindrical-shaped boiler. Instead, this engine

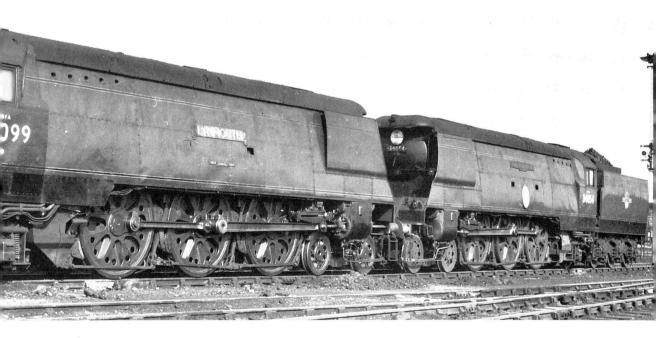

was clad with streamlined metal plating, presenting to the eye a shape which some detractors suggested bore resemblance to a tin of Spam, hence the nickname 'Spam-cans'. Many bore upon their sides the coat of arms and name of a town or city, or a well-known landmark of south Wiltshire, Somerset, Devon, Dorset or Cornwall, counties through which they might be seen working. This gave rise to their more respectful name, the 'West Country' class. Other engines of the same class carried names to commemorate the Battle of Britain. A similar, but larger and more powerful design of locomotive hauled the heaviest of the express trains between Waterloo and Exeter or Bournemouth. These were the 'Merchant Navy' class of Pacifics, all named after shipping lines which used the Southern Railway ports at Southampton and elsewhere. Some years later, starting in 1956, many of these engines were to be rebuilt, the most obvious change being the removal of the streamlined or, as it was officially known, air-smoothed casings, and their replacement with conventional cladding. But when I first visited Salisbury, many of these engines were but a few years old, and such changes were a thing of the future.

After that first visit, I returned home to report my findings to fellow enthusiasts, most of them members of the local church choir who, during the Sunday sermon, passed notes of locomotives seen at various lineside locations during the previous week. My new enthusiasm for the Southern Railway, and in particular for the Bulleid Pacifics, was met with hoots of derision from some of the older boys. On reflection, I should have known better than to extol the virtues of a 'foreign' line, for locospotters were notorious for their prejudice towards the railway company that served the area in which they were born and brought up. In my home town, any boy who showed the remotest interest in railways soon learnt that there was only one railway worthy of study – and that was the Great Western. I suppose this was only natural, for just 30 miles up the road was to be found the birthplace of Great Western 'Kings', 'Castles' and the like – the great railway workshops of Swindon.

I had already developed a wider interest in railway motive power, and I must have persuaded at least some of my friends likewise, because I recall that Salisbury became the venue for the occasional Saturday locospotting excursion, watching the passage of holiday trains to and from the West Country. It was even worth enduring the mocking comments of my friends as yet another of my favourite Bulleid Pacifics lost its grip on the rail, displaying

TOP RIGHT *The Swindon look. This traditional* G W R *design constrasted sharply with the new look of the Southern Pacifics.*

the propensity to 'pick up her feet' while attempting to restart a heavy train bound for Waterloo. I recall how once, a member of the station staff went to great lengths to explain to us that the driver of the train we had just witnessed experiencing problems with getting his train underway must have been 'a Brighton man'. 'You don't see locomotives handled like that by South Western men,' the porter advised. Thereafter, and displaying great authority, whenever we witnessed wheelslip from a Southern locomotive, one or more of us would confidently announce to anyone who might be listening that the driver was 'a Brighton man'! No doubt, at Brighton, those enthusiasts who witnessed a Bulleid Pacific experiencing similar problems with loss of adhesion were being advised by some equally partisan member of staff that the driver was in all probability 'a Salisbury man'.

All trains, with but two exceptions, halted at Salisbury station, many changing crews and taking on water. The exceptions were the westbound, and the corresponding eastbound, working of the all-Pullman 'Devon Belle' which was advertised as non-stop in each direction between London and Sidmouth Junction. I soon learnt, however, that the 'Belle' made an unadvertised halt at Wilton, 2 miles west of Salisbury, to change engines. The passage of the 'Devon Belle', even at slow speed through Salisbury station, was a fine sight, the immaculate engine heading 12, or even 14 Pullman coaches including, at the rear, a special observation coach (which today runs at a more sedate speed alongside the River Dart, between Totnes and Buckfastleigh, on the preserved Dart Valley Railway).

Sadly, the 'Devon Belle' ran for only a few years, for despite initial success the service failed to attract enough passengers, perhaps because no real attempt was made to match the speed of the rival service from Paddington, over the ex-G W R line, to Exeter.

Far more successful over the Southern route was the ACE – the 'Atlantic Coast Express' – which made its début in 1926 as a titled train, but which had run as an unnamed express for many years before. During the week, and on out-of-season Saturdays, the ACE earned the title of the most multi-portioned train in the land, conveying through coaches between Waterloo and the Atlantic coast resorts of Ilfracombe, Bideford and Torrington, together with other coaches to Seaton, Sidmouth, Exmouth and Plymouth. But on summer Saturdays, such was the volume of railborne holiday traffic in the 1950s – the final

ABOVE *The 'Ace' leaving Salisbury for Exeter in October 1961.*
RIGHT *A Drummond M7 class tank shunts a parcels van at Salisbury station.*

years before the boom in private car ownership – that the number of travellers to each resort would often swell the demand for seats from a single coach to a complete train. As a result, on such Saturdays, one could witness many a train with the title 'Atlantic Coast Express' pausing at Salisbury. In addition, of course, the cross-country route via the ex-Great Western line carried frequent trains between Cardiff or Bristol and the south coast.

Eastbound trains from the Bristol direction arrived at Salisbury behind an ex-Great Western 'Hall' or 'Grange' – sometimes perhaps a 'Castle' or 'County' class locomotive – the copper-topped chimneys and shining brass-work contrasting with the Southern engines which lacked such decoration. After coming to a halt at the platform, the GW engine would be uncoupled from her train, and run forward to be diverted on to another line. Her place was taken by a Southern engine, which would back down on to the train to be coupled up ready for the continuation of the journey. Meanwhile, the GW engine would head off back through the station, to be turned and made ready at the large locomotive depot for a return working to Bristol or beyond.

Between all this activity, the station shunter, usually an elderly ex-London & South Western Drummond class M7, or an 0–6–0 class G6, could be seen fussing about, collecting empty coaches to add to the rear of a London-bound train, or waiting at the east end of the station for the arrival of a down 'Atlantic Coast Express', for at Salisbury the rear coaches bound for Seaton would be detached from the main train. As soon as the ACE had departed, the Seaton

coaches would be shunted on to the rear of another westbound train – a semi-fast service calling at intermediate stations, including, of course, Seaton Junction, where the through coaches for Seaton would be transferred yet again, this time to the local branch train to run the final few miles to their destination by the sea.

Inevitably, at some time during the day, somebody amongst our gang would suggest a visit to the nearby locomotive depot. We all knew before we set off from the station that any attempt to steal into the 'shed' was doomed to failure, but this never seemed to deter yet another attempt. The depot, which on a summer Saturday would at times be positively seething with engines, had only one entrance from the road, and this lay up a narrow flight of steps in the back corner of the depot. From the pavement could be seen no more than a tantalising glimpse of what lay within this Aladdin's cave. But try taking more than a couple of paces up those steps, and from a small office within came the stern voice of the foreman, telling the uninvited, in no uncertain terms, to 'Get out'! On the way back to the station, we took turns to hoist one another high enough to attempt just a fleeting glimpse of locomotives which could be heard in the yard on the opposite side of a high brick wall.

ABOVE *Eighty-four years of history separate this Beattie Well tank of 1874*
from the massive '9F' of 1958 beside it at Salisbury shed.
BELOW *Southern steam at Salisbury shed with 'West Country' No. 34099*
'Lynmouth' on the left, 'S15' No. 30827, 'H15' No. 30522 and 'U' No. 31804.

OPPOSITE *A glimpse of the locomotives from outside the foreman's office, Salisbury.*
ABOVE *'Merchant Navy' No. 35028 'Clan Line' has its smokebox emptied at Weymouth shed, 1965.*

Perhaps it was the sight of all the holiday trains that tempted me to explore the old L&SWR system, beyond the immediate environs of Salisbury station. My interest in railways was developing beyond the stage of mere 'number-taking'. In any event, the financial reward of nine shillings (45p) per week for undertaking a daily paper round enabled me to plan the occasional trip down the main line west of Salisbury. It took only one such journey, and like many before me, I was hooked by this exciting section of main line.

The feature which endeared the line to enthusiasts was its switchback nature, and superb alignment. Running east to west, and parallel to the coast, the route was forced to cut across the natural lie of the land, climbing hard to surmount the watershed of one river valley before tumbling downhill into the next valley. And so, all the way from south Wiltshire, through Somerset and Dorset, the line continuously climbed and fell towards Devon. But so well was it laid out that, in steam days, once past Wilton, just to the west of Salisbury, there was not a single speed restriction for the remainder of the journey to Exeter. As a result, the long and heavy holiday trains could take the fullest advantage of the down grades and, running very fast, gain sufficient momentum to attack the next bank in fine style. The best place to observe such trains, of

ABOVE *West Country No. 34024 'Tamar Valley' comes over the summit at Buckhorn Weston with a Waterloo train in August 1958.*

RIGHT *Two Great Western tanks on the Southern main line at Axminster in 1965.*

38

course, was at the foot of each 'dip', where speed would be at a maximum – often somewhere between 80 and 90mph. The never-to-be-forgotten sight of a Bulleid Pacific in 'full cry', with her train of 12 or more matching green coaches hammering down the bank on a sunny summer day . . . what memories!

Axminster, the first station after passing the boundary into Devon, lay close to the bottom of a long descent, after which the Exeter-bound express faced the most severe test on the entire run from Salisbury. This is the infamous Seaton bank, a 7-mile climb culminating in the passage through Honiton tunnel. So at Axminster, westbound trains may be travelling between 80 and 90mph, gathering as much impetus as possible to attack the long climb up to Honiton tunnel. Similarly, eastbound trains, after the rapid descent of Seaton bank, pass through Axminster station at only a little less speed than their westbound counterparts as they commence the climb towards Crewkerne.

Axminster was one of those places which, with hindsight, I wished I had visited more often. In addition to seeing the high-speed running of the express trains, the station was the junction for a delightful 7-mile branch line, first opened in 1903, which wriggled its way back across the Devon/Dorset boundary to the small but popular seaside resort of Lyme Regis.

Having been approved as a Light Railway, the construction of the line was less substantial than would otherwise have been the case. The result was a line of steep gradients and a meandering course as the track climbed up around the rolling countryside to reach a destination which, as the crow flew, was but $4\frac{1}{4}$ miles. This combination of heavy gradients and sharp curves was the cause of some concern, as in early days various types of locomotives were unsuccessfully tried out over the line. But from 1916 one class of engine, the Adams 4–4–2 'Radial' tanks built in the 1880s, held undisputed sway on the branch. By the late 1950s these grand old ladies, who should, perhaps, have long since retired, were still to be found working the branch line, attracting growing numbers of enthusiasts to photograph their work, especially on summer Saturdays when two such engines might be seen working in tandem.

During the week, the branch train trundled to and fro between Axminster and Lyme, but the real interest to the enthusiast occurred on summer Saturdays when there were several through workings between Waterloo and Lyme

ABOVE *A Waterloo–Exmouth dives into Honiton tunnel in August 1964.*

RIGHT *Nos. 30584 and 30583 catch the evening sun as they double-head the 6.45 from Axminster to Lyme Regis, 6 June 1960.*

Regis. Early in the morning, the engine which was to work the branch line for the following week would arrive at Axminster having travelled up the main line from the large locomotive depot at Exmouth Junction, on the outskirts of Exeter. During the day, this engine would 'double up' with the engine which had worked the branch train during the current week, and together they would pull trains which included through carriages between London and Lyme Regis. These carriages were detached from, or added to, the main-line trains at Axminster. At the end of the day's through workings, the locomotive which had worked the branch train for the preceding week set off for a well-earned rest at Exmouth Junction, where she would receive any necessary attention before returning to Axminster the following Saturday, to change places yet again with her sister engine.

These old Adams 'Radial' tank engines lasted until 1961, when they were finally ousted from the branch line by more modern steam power. Thankfully, one of the Adams tanks was saved and today can be seen many miles from her old haunts, working on the Bluebell Railway in Sussex. In 1963 the branch service was 'dieselised' and just two years later the little line closed.

To the west of Axminster, the main line crosses the river Axe before turning north-west out of the valley and commencing the long, hard slog up Seaton bank, passing a patchwork of little fields and scattered farms, each with

its own cider orchard. The hamlets of this eastern corner of Devon are joined by a network of narrow, winding lanes, the routes of which often lie hidden behind steep banks and high hedges. South of Cotleigh, the line enters a deep wooded cutting before diving into the inky black bore of Honiton tunnel.

As the railway reaches towards the eastern outskirts of Exeter it passes the site of the large motive-power depot at Exmouth Junction, once home to more than 100 locomotives, for Exeter was the hub of the Southern Railway's West Country services. The line passes a large marshalling yard before plunging down through Black Boys tunnel, making for Exeter Central, a most impressive station dating from a major rebuilding undertaken by the Southern Railway in 1933.

At Exeter Central, trains from Waterloo which carried through coaches for Plymouth, north Cornwall and north Devon were divided to be taken

ABOVE *No. 30584, an Adams tank, at Wyke Green on the Lyme Regis branch.*
RIGHT *By 1968 steam was gone and Western Region management had reduced the important Salisbury–Exeter main-line route to a single track.*

forward by semi-fast or local trains. In the reverse direction, the separate portions were combined into a single train for Waterloo. But, as mentioned earlier, on summer Saturdays, separate complete trains were often required to handle the volume of traffic to and from resorts which, on weekdays, might provide only a handful of passengers. In the early 1950s, for example, eastbound express trains departed from Exeter for Salisbury or beyond at 10.00a.m., 10.15, 10.30, 11.05, 11.25, 11.40, 11.55, 12.10p.m., 12.30, 12.45, 1.00, 1.30, 1.42, and 2.10. A similar number of trains ran to Exeter in the reverse direction, and in the midst of this heavy traffic, room had to be found for local and branch trains.

Such volumes of traffic continued to run on summer Saturdays throughout the 1950s – years which were to prove the post-war zenith of the old L&SW line to Exeter. How many enthusiasts, like myself, realised that what they were witnessing would, within a decade, so change that the very existence of the Salisbury–Exeter main line would be under threat? By the late 1950s the diesel locomotive was already holding sway on the rival route of the old GW line between London, Exeter and the West Country. And how ironic that, at a time

when so many diesel-hauled services were seeing little overall improvement in speed or timekeeping, the Southern Region, in 1961, announced that the steam-hauled 'Atlantic Coast Express' was to be accelerated to reach Exeter from Waterloo in less than three hours! 1964 heralded a reorganisation by British Railways which handed control of all Southern lines west of Salisbury to the Western Region, the 'successor' to the old enemy – the Great Western. Soon came an announcement of plans to concentrate all through traffic to the west beyond Exeter via the old Great Western route.

During the first weekend in September 1964, the last regular express passenger trains over the Salisbury–Exeter line were steam-hauled. On Monday 6 September 1964, a diesel-hauled, semi-fast service commenced running between Waterloo, Salisbury and Exeter. The best time from London to Exeter, albeit with more intermediate stops, was three hours thirty-five minutes, forty minutes slower than the steam-hauled ACE of just three years earlier. At the same time came an announcement of proposals to close ten stations and, with the exception of the Exmouth line, every branch service between Salisbury and Exeter. The main line was to be reduced, for much of its length, to single track, the single line sections extending from Wilton to Templecombe, and from Yeovil Junction to Pinhoe. The London & South Western route had become a sad shadow of its former self.

Today, more than 20 years later, Southern Region has at last regained control over its old main line, which now forms a part of the Network South East system. Even if, in BR parlance, 'South East' has been somewhat liberally interpreted to include a line extending as far westwards as Exeter, at least the Salisbury to Exeter route is once again within the control of a caring area management eager to promote the line and to provide a proper public service. Stations at Templecombe, Seaton Junction (now renamed Feniton), and Pinhoe, although now with only basic facilities, have been reopened. Buildings have been repainted in the bright new Network South East livery. At Salisbury, the main entrance has even been redecorated in the colours and style of the old L&SWR. A new passing loop has been installed at Tisbury to break up the long single line section between Wilton and Gillingham, while the line between Salisbury and Yeovil has been used for special trains, hauled once again by steam, with the restored Bulleid Pacific, 'Merchant Navy' class No. 35028 *Clan Line*, returning once again to her old haunts.

RIGHT *M7 tank No. 30060 near Furzebrook with the branch-line train from Swanage to Wareham in May 1961.*

44

Southern steam can also be found on the Mid-Hants railway, otherwise known as the Watercress Line, which runs from the delightful Hampshire town of Alresford to connect to the British Rail system at Alton. Once part of a cross-country line linking Woking to Winchester, its gradients were of such severity that railwaymen referred to one section as taking a trip 'over the Alps'. The superb restoration scheme has included the complete relaying of the track, which had been lifted following closure by BR.

Further west, into Dorset, lies another ex-L & SW line where substantial work continues towards restoration. This is the ten-mile branch line which ran from Wareham, across the Isle of Purbeck, passing through Corfe Castle to Swanage. In recent years, and against all odds, the Swanage Railway Project has been slowly rebuilding the line from the restored terminus at Swanage.

This line to Swanage was familiar territory to me, and I still have vivid memories of the shrill whistle of a Drummond M7 tank echoing across the

valley shortly after dusk on a summer's evening in the 1950s. The whistle was to remind the signalman – and most of the town's occupants – that the last train of the day from Wareham was approaching the station at Swanage. The clanking 0–4–4 tank engine, pushing two elderly L&SWR coaches before it over the final mile of its journey, would whistle its approach nightly at around 10.40p.m.

The bonus that came with a weekend visit to Swanage in the 1950s was the summer Saturday traffic which worked along the line. On such days, the single line from Wareham really came to life, with the arrival and departure of through trains to and from Waterloo when main-line engines worked over the single-line branch to the terminus. Then it was possible to witness workings not normally seen at the end of a ten-mile country branch line.

Just to the west of the station, an overbridge spanned the railway in Northbrook Road. This offered a wonderful vantage point, for from the parapet on one side I could see across the entire station complex and the various sidings which fanned out into the goods yard. From the opposite parapet of the bridge I could look down on the small engine shed which, each night, housed the locomotive employed on the branch push and pull train. 'Push and pull' because the engine pushed its coaches from Wareham to Swanage, and pulled them back to Wareham.

On summer Saturdays the station sidings were invariably filled with coaching stock which would see use later in the day. Prominent in the fore-

ABOVE *The view from Northbrook Road bridge in Swanage: Ivatt tank No. 41316.*

ground stood the signal box, close enough for the bell-codes exchanged with the box at Corfe Castle to be heard clearly, providing the signalman had slid open the end window in his box. Behind the box stood a large goods shed which, on weekdays, was still reasonably busy. Beyond the goods shed lay Swanage station, with one long platform complete with a run-round loop, and a shorter bay platform.

On the Corfe Castle side of the overbridge, in front of the engine shed, there was a 50ft turntable – far too short to accommodate the Bulleid Pacifics which would visit the line regularly during those summer weekends. The line to Corfe curved away into the distance, accompanied on one side by a long siding which had once provided access to a small stone yard. The bridge over the line was therefore the ideal position from which all of the railway activity at Swanage could be observed.

My arrival at the bridge on a Saturday morning was often timed to coincide with the arrival of the 8.18a.m. local from Wareham which would be hauled by a Bulleid Pacific, running tender-first. The 'West Country' class locomotive would dispose of its lightweight load before retiring to the goods yard where it would collect a set of ten carriages to form the 9.15a.m. departure to Waterloo. Also to be seen in the goods yard was the Swanage pilot engine, sent down specially from Bournemouth to shunt the stock of incoming trains and release train engines from the buffer stops – the length of the incoming trains from London precluding use of the run-round loop. The station pilot would be one of the elderly Drummond '700' class 0–6–0s, known as 'Black Motors', or occasionally a Maunsell 'Q' class 0–6–0.

Following the arrival and subsequent departure of the local push and pull train, the Pacific would haul out on to the main line the empty coaching stock (which had been brought down to Swanage late the previous night), before reversing back into the station. Departure at 9.15a.m. was guaranteed to raise the echoes as the Bulleid struggled to find her feet on the adverse gradient, but it also provided the unusual sight of a train setting off against the starting signal, the length of the train demanding that the engine stand well in advance of the platform starter which the signalman was physically prevented from pulling to 'line clear'.

After the 9.15 had left there would be a lull of some 50 minutes, before the arrival of the next local train. The wait was, however, worthwhile, as it sometimes presented the rare sight of a two-coach train hauled by *two* engines – the branch engine piloted by a tender-first Bulleid Pacific, the latter being brought down from Bournemouth to work the next through train to Waterloo.

Sometimes the Bulleid preceded the push and pull train, working light engine into Swanage, having apparently arrived at Wareham piloting the 5.40a.m. Waterloo to Weymouth train from Bournemouth Central.

As with the 9.15a.m. through train, the stock for the 11.34a.m. departure to Waterloo had to be collected from the goods yard, where it had lain idle since the previous Saturday. The 11.34 was joined at Wareham by the 11.00 from Weymouth, the combined train then working forward via Hamworthy, Broadstone, Wimborne and Ringwood, thereby avoiding the Bournemouth area. This circuitous route was the course of the original Southampton & Dorchester Railway promoted by a local solicitor, A.L. Castleman, and was referred to as 'Castleman's Corkscrew'. In more reverent terms, however, the route was often referred to as 'the Old Road', and was a useful diversion to relieve the intensive traffic running over the Bournemouth–Poole section on summer Saturdays well into the early 1960s.

Shortly after 12.30p.m., the first of the incoming through trains from London would arrive at Swanage, again hauled by a Bulleid Pacific running tender-first. This engine would work light from Bournemouth to Wareham, where it took over the haulage of the 9.15a.m. from Waterloo for the final ten miles across the Isle of Purbeck.

Following the departure of the 12.40p.m. local to Wareham, the station pilot would couple on to the rear of the 9.15a.m. ex-Waterloo and, often with great difficulty, draw out the empty stock to release the train engine. The stock was then returned to the platform, enabling the 'West Country' to back on to the head of the train to form the 1.23p.m. departure to Waterloo. As with the 11.34a.m., this train was routed via 'the Old Road' to avoid Bournemouth.

At 2.10p.m. the second of the through trains from Waterloo arrived at Swanage behind the inevitable Bulleid Pacific. Once again the station pilot would stir into action, and following departure of the local train to Wareham, would remove the empty stock from the platform line. The rake of carriages would be set back into the station yard, where it would remain to form the 11.34a.m. train to Waterloo the next Saturday.

The Bulleid Pacific, freed of its train, would return 'light-engine' to Bournemouth, but not before the arrival of the 2.42p.m. local from Wareham. The enforced wait did, however, permit a visit to the water tower, the engine pulling up just beyond the parapet of the road bridge, a 'bird's-eye view'.

TOP RIGHT *M7 No. 30060 pushes its train out of Wareham towards Swanage. The driver is in the leading coach, his controls linked by rods to the locomotive.*

The eventual departure of the 'West Country' usually signalled the end of my visit, for the remainder of the day's operations involved only the pair of push and pull sets working the branch trains. This included the working of through carriages from Waterloo, attached to the local at Wareham – including coaches from 'The Royal Wessex', another named express complete with carriage destination boards. But after the excitement of the earlier through trains, the comings and goings of the branch-line local trains seemed too dull to warrant my further attention.

Just a few years ago, I thought I would never again get the chance to sit on the parapet of the Northbrook Road bridge, to listen to the clanking sound of a Drummond M7 tank, or to see a Bulleid Pacific. Only two class M7 tanks survived – one locked away in the National Railway collection, the other residing half a world away, exported to a railway museum in Pennsylvania, USA. But, to my great delight, in early April 1987 this engine was 'home' again, having been repurchased and brought back across the Atlantic to Swanage, arriving exactly 23 years after she last steamed out of Swanage, heading for Corfe and Wareham. Two Bulleid Pacifics are also to be based at Swanage following restoration, and soon it should be possible to travel once again across Purbeck over a typical London & South Western Railway branch line. Happily, South Western memories live on.

The Dinorwic slate quarry was worked in a series of galleries rising one above the other up the mountainside. Here 'Dolbadarn' squeezes out of a short and very tight tunnel.

INDUSTRIAL
RAILWAYS

—∘3∘—

ERIC TONKS

Some years ago in the library at Melton Mowbray I saw a small booklet for sale entitled *The Story of Stoney Stanton* (a village in Leicestershire near the Warwickshire border). Fifty, even thirty, years ago, such a book would have had a picture of the church or the house of one of the landed gentry on the cover. This was different – it had a picture of an elderly locomotive shunting at the local granite quarries. Like jazz, industrial locomotives and railways are now respectable and accepted as worthy of serious study and recording. The point was that, while a main line locomotive could be seen in a dozen counties, this one could be positively identified with its place of work as part of local history.

The term 'industrial railways' broadly includes all railways owned by industry, the most familiar being those by which coal is moved from the pithead to the main-line railway system; or hazardous chemicals are taken from manufacturer to user. The materials are transported in bulk, in wagons specially designed for their purpose, moving at express speeds through the BR network. At both ends of the main-line journey the industrial railway comes into its own, where the wagons are moved by the factory owner's private locomotives. These are all diesel now, of course, and fairly standardised, but industrial railways have a more exciting, and individualistic, past.

Industrial railways predate passenger railways by some three centuries. The earliest railways were all industrial, laid down to speed the transport of minerals over land where roads were poor or non-existent. They carried ore from mines in the mountains, coal from the pits, stone from quarries on the moors. These first railways were often called tramways and were mostly short lines, taking their loads to the nearest navigable river or canal, as at that time water was the principal means of conveying material any distance. Some longer lines were put down where topographical difficulties ruled out canals.

Wooden rails sufficed for the earliest industrial railways, but soon iron rails became universal. Sleepers could be of wood or – very often in upland districts – stone blocks slotted to receive rails. Some of these early stone sleeper blocks have survived, and can still be seen today in remote areas; the wooden sleepers have, of course, long since disappeared. While there is no hard and fast definition, the stone-block lines were generally referred to as tramroads, the others as wagonways. Each line was built by or for the owners of a quarry or mine, and a wayleave would be arranged with the owner of the land over which the lines were to run. Horse traction was general, though on very short lines the wagons were pushed by men; but at the beginning of the nineteenth century came the first steam locomotives, designed solely for use on some of the industrial lines that had by then come into use.

The most obvious impact of the introduction of locomotives was the complete transformation it brought to passenger transport everywhere, but its effect on the movement of goods was earlier and no less dramatic. The difference was that before the Rainhill Trials of 1829 there were to all intents and purposes no passenger-carrying railways, whereas there were railways of a kind for carrying minerals and merchandise, including a few public companies such as the Surrey Iron Railway of 1801. As the main-line railways rapidly transformed transport in the Victorian era, the old tramroads mostly disappeared. Those with the greatest traffic potential, such as the lines serving the collieries in the north-east of England and in south Wales, were altered and absorbed into the railway system as mineral branches or as industrial feeder systems operated by the colliery owners. Tramroads elsewhere mostly fell into disuse, but a few survived almost unchanged well into the twentieth century, as in the Forest of Dean. From the mid-nineteenth century, the majority of industrial railways became adjuncts of the main-line railways, as most of industry switched its traffic to rail and away from the canals.

The spread of the railway system encouraged the exploitation of mineral resources close to the line. This was a reversal of the original concept of railways as being built to serve areas where there was need of them. Now, industry was developed because there was already a railway line to bring in raw materials and take away finished products.

The distinct identity of the industrial railway was emphasised by the introduction, in about 1860, of locomotives specially designed for industrial use. Hitherto, most private owners of locomotives were forced to be content with locomotives of main-line type, usually secondhand, which were unsuitable for works shunting where the track was often of light rail and the curves sharp. Up to this time, the only alternative for private owners was to build their own engines. In the 1860s a number of firms started building locomotives specifically for industrial work and their products spread all over Britain, and indeed the world.

With the steam locomotive recognised as the most effective method of haulage, development proceeded apace, but with a pleasing lack of uniformity – a characteristic that attracted enthusiasts as main-line railways became more standardised. Different industries imposed their individual stamps on private railway development, and though for the most part they were content to buy locomotives ready made by established manufacturers, there were many examples of locomotives designed for specific locations or strongly associated with them. In many ways, too, transport was a local affair dictated by the ingenuity and purse of the owner, giving each system an individual character.

Private railways were built to serve a wide variety of industries, with coal taking pride of place. Some of the earlier railways had rails of various odd gauges handed down from wagonways; otherwise most of the lines were laid to the railway standard 4ft 8½ins gauge. Ironworks, foundries and the like, followed in due time by gasworks, power stations and a wide variety of manufacturing premises, had lines of this gauge, with direct physical connection to the main railway.

Minerals, on the other hand, did not always lie so conveniently, and longer railway lines were needed to connect the quarries to the railway or to the works for processing; hence the widespread use of narrow-gauge track that was cheaper to lay and maintain. The cost of the extra manpower required for the transfer of the minerals was of relatively minor significance in those days.

The most popular type of steam locomotive for industrial work was the saddle tank, carrying its water in a saddle-shaped tank over the boiler. Wheels were usually four- or six-coupled, depending on the kind of track and the loads to be hauled. Within this restricted framework there was ample scope for variety, with locomotives of different sizes; and even makers' 'standard' locomotives often developed individual characteristics when in industrial use, either unintentionally or by design to meet special local requirements. Some tramways passed through low tunnels, so the engines had cut-down cabs and

TOP *Industrial locomotives came in all shapes and sizes, but this Garratt articulated locomotive at Baddesley Colliery was the largest and the most powerful.*

ABOVE *Few standard-gauge engines in industry were smaller or older than this Lewin tank of 1863, which worked at Seaham Harbour.*

TOP *Most industrials were saddle tanks with six or four coupled wheels. These two examples at Measham Colliery were typical.*
ABOVE *Rawnsley Colliery employed this engine which had been bought secondhand from main-line service. She was built by the London, Brighton and South Coast Railway in 1877.*

boiler mountings like chimneys and domes, and even, so it is said, used small drivers! Other lines had narrow tunnels, so the locomotives had open-back cabs to enable the crew to escape should the engine become derailed in the tunnel. The differing policies of the owners were apparent. Some believed in buying new equipment and scrapping the old to keep moving with the times. Others patched up the old to cut expenses.

History played its part in shaping industrial railways too. There had been ironstone quarries at Desborough in Northamptonshire since the coming of the Midland Railway in 1857, and from the turn of the century one of them was operated by the Co-op – the only ironstone line the Co-operative movement ever ran. These quarries, like many others, were closed in the post-First World War slump, but were later reopened by a different company, who used the ore not to make iron but as a pigment and in chemical processing. For this purpose the ore had to be reduced to a fine powder, and a brown haze continually hung over the plant, earning it the title of 'the snuff factory'. Ore was brought to the works in narrow-gauge wagons hauled by 'Prince' – a horse, not a locomotive – and was there crushed, sorted, bagged and loaded on to a wagon for transit to BR.

ABOVE *When Ivo Peters photographed this engine at one of the Desborough ironstone mines in 1960, she had been derelict for several years and all traces of her true identity had vanished.*

The track on the branch was appalling. Perhaps it had never been renewed since 1904, when it was first laid down, but more likely it had been re-laid with secondhand rail just good enough to get by. On the 'straight' sections the rails were badly aligned vertically and laterally, while the sharply curved portion consisted of a series of very short lengths of straight rail over which the driver pulled the solitary wagon very gingerly indeed. The cutting was a running stream, as it passed over a spring between the rails, which did not help maintenance but grew excellent watercress. On one side of the cutting were the garden fences of houses backing on to the railway, and as these were in constant danger of falling on the track, they were supported by timbers at various angles, several of them straddling the tramway. A footplate trip was not comfortable but certainly unforgettable. The extraordinary thing was that the ramshackle atmosphere was not a hangover from the past but had been created in modern times from 1920 to 1967, when the line was closed. The genial 'gaffer' would let visitors look around, unaware of any imperfections.

The narrow-gauge lines had a charm of their own, particularly those in open country; while the limitations in design imposed by the gauge made the locomotives of special interest. The term 'narrow gauge' covers lines of less than the standard 4ft 8½ins, and the commonest were 2ft and 3ft; but there were odd gauges, such as 2ft 8½ins, that mostly derived from the pre-locomotive era of horse traction, when the operator simply put down rails and built wagons to suit the terrain and the loads. Locomotive designs were flexible, so that engines of the same mechanical dimensions could be adapted to suit a variety of gauges.

The names given to industrial locomotives cover a wide range, but every name had some significance. Place names were common – villages near the place of work, or small geographical features. Boys' and girls' names were common too, particularly interesting if you can find out *which* Joan or Betty is meant. Where large locomotive fleets were in use, as at the major steelworks and some of the larger collieries, the owners usually found it more convenient for operating purposes to give the locomotives numbers; in so doing they were following the practice of the main-line railways. Even so, some still kept to names, as at Bilston and Shelton ironworks in Staffordshire. One chemical works used elements (*Sodium*, for example) as a source of names, and a Warwickshire cement works relied on geological names such as *Mesozoic*.

But there is more to industrial railways than just the rails and the loco-motives; each factory or quarry layout was a complete railway in itself, fully involved in factory processes as part of an integrated system.

ABOVE 'Blanche' on a wooded stretch of the Penrhyn Railway in 1956. This narrow-gauge line linked the Penrhyn slate quarries with the North Wales coast. 'Blanche' survives on the preserved Festiniog Railway.

TOP RIGHT Boy meets girl: 'Sybil' and 'George B' pause briefly for a group photo with their drivers on the narrow-gauge system at Dinorwic slate quarries.

The enviable record of rail as the safest form of travel has been achieved by the adoption of a strict code of practice built up by long experience in public service. Industrial railways are in quite a different category, being on private property. Initially, there was little recognition of the special hazards associated with railway operation, and Victorian newspapers record numerous accidents to workers. In due course, industrial railways, along with other aspects of safety at work, came under the jurisdiction of the Factory Inspector.

Industrial railways were closer to grass-roots level and their long history ensured the retention of simpler (or just different) forms of operation not found on the main lines. For instance, signalling was not usual, and train movements were very much in the hands of men on the spot. Sometimes a crude telegraph system would be installed, with lineside calling-up points for drivers seeking permission to proceed. The larger systems had to introduce more in the way of rules but were free to do so in their own way.

A few terms almost entirely specific to industrial railways have arisen from this freedom. 'Shunters' on main lines become 'rope runners' in industry, from the days when rope was in common use for wagon movement. Narrow-gauge wagons released from the cable after descending an incline were brought to a halt by having a bar of iron or hard wood thrust through the spokes; this tool was called a 'sprag' and the wielder of it would be given the nickname. 'Fly shunting' – placing wagons on a different line by switching the points after the main part of the train had passed over – was another fairly common practice.

Drivers of industrial locomotives probably included no more in the way of 'characters' than their counterparts on the main lines, but long association with a small system, the same few engines, and a minimum of 'rules' tended to underline any eccentricities. Visitors to Newlyn in Cornwall up to the 1950s can hardly have failed to see a rather odd-looking narrow-gauge locomotive, with tall chimney and cab, pulling a string of wagons laden with granite to the quayside. Only recently has this engine been identified as one built in 1901 by an obscure German maker. How she came to Newlyn no one could remember, but possibly she had been used by the Germans at the front in the First World War and afterwards was included in miscellaneous reparations. At Newlyn she was in the charge of a driver older than her – and she was his life. He drove her, cleaned her and looked after her as a mother cares for her baby; and no one else dared to touch her. He would work at weekends to keep her going. If you called at a time when she was requiring mechanical attention you would find a row of tools and parts dotted along the footplate – and woe betide anyone who shifted anything!

Eventually, in 1950, came the day when the ageing boiler was declared beyond economic repair and *Penlee* (as she was called) was confined to the shed, her duties undertaken by more efficient diesel locomotives. Each day her driver would call at the shed, musing over his former charge and fiddling uselessly with the motion; but he did not long outlive her as, literally, he had nothing else to live for. The management, well aware of the strong link between

TOP RIGHT *'Penlee' on the dockside at Newlyn in Cornwall, where she was photographed by an early enthusiast. After half a century of working life, much of it shared with one devoted driver, the locomotive was retired from service.*

man and machine, gave *Penlee* a coat of paint and put her on a plinth by the sea wall for interested visitors to see; for indeed she had become a local celebrity. But the salt spray soon played havoc with the new paintwork and reduced her to a rusty hulk. Associated Roadstone Corporation had by this time taken over the quarry and, with the benevolence these giant corporations can sometimes show, arranged for her to be taken to their training workshops in Oxfordshire for restoration. She has now been done up, but sadly she is not likely to return to Cornwall for a reunion with the spirit of her old driver.

From the 1920s a few enthusiasts, particularly photographers, became interested in industrial locomotives, but for the most part they concentrated on the locomotives as such and, with honourable exceptions, did not take many

TOP *A clever combination of steam shunter and steam crane produced the 'crane tank'. These worked at William Doxford's shipyard in Sunderland.*

ABOVE *Two generations of steam at the Philadelphia coal stage on the Lambton collieries railway in County Durham. No. 5, an ex-Taff Vale Railway veteran of 1899, stands in front of No. 8, built in 1952.*

'action' shots of locomotives against their industrial background. Films were even rarer, so we must treasure the efforts of dedicated enthusiasts such as Ivo Peters to capture the spirit of these small railways.

Industrial railways were to be found throughout the land, but with the greatest concentration in coal-mining and iron- and steel-making areas. In addition, there were engineering works of all kinds, chemical plants, tar works and others. There were service industries such as docks, gasworks, water-works and power stations, and lighter industry such as biscuit and chocolate manufacturers. These were mainly in urban surroundings, though some col-lieries were well away from towns; but there were plenty of industrial railways in rural areas, mostly associated with quarrying activities for minerals – slate, granite, iron ore, china clay, limestone and gypsum (beside the last two were usually cement and plaster works respectively). Then there were metal mines, sand and gravel pits, brickworks and peat bogs. A large proportion of these rural sites boasted the additional attraction of narrow-gauge tramways. Finally, there were a few industrial lines connected with agriculture, notably the numerous sugar factories of the east Midlands; while minor lines served potato farms, watercress beds and the like. One category of industrial railway that defies ready classification was the noisome 'rubbish shoot' railways that spread London's domestic refuse over the Essex marshes before the days of specialised lorries for this task. While necessarily in open country, they hardly qualified as attractive environments in any weather.

If locomotives were there, then interested enthusiasts would pay them visits – and these jaunts took them into some remote areas, improving their geography if nothing else. A friend of mine, now dead, alas, used to travel by motorbike to the more inaccessible spots. He never bothered to carry any maps but relied on signposts and the 'locals'. On one occasion he was looking for a minor line at Pont Neath Vaughan in south-east Wales. It was some time before he realised that Pont Nedd Fechan was the same place!

Collieries, ironworks and foundries were by their very nature grubby places, and it was not easy for the locomotive crews to keep their engines in pristine condition. But they did their best, and any shortcomings in appearance were often transcended by interesting design features. It is surprising how much variation was possible between locomotives originally of identical build, once they had been in service a few years. A works might have, say, six locomotives of the same class, but it is usually possible to identify each engine by a different whistle, an addition to the cab, or a dent on the frame from a minor accident.

As coals are proverbially associated with Newcastle, so is brewing with Burton upon Trent. Motorists who regularly travelled through the town not all that many years ago will remember the frequent hold-ups at the level crossings where brewery railways crossed, and perhaps their impatience was mitigated somewhat by the sight of smartly kept little engines as, with bell ringing, they chuffed cheerfully across. They were always in sparkling condition in the liveries of their owners – brick red (Bass), royal blue and gold (Worthington), mid green (Marston, Thomson and Evershed), and dark green (Ind Coope). Their gleaming paintwork and polished brass fittings brought a touch of colour to the rather drab streets. North of the border the distilleries of Scotland kept their engines in similarly immaculate condition, with here the added bonus of mountain backgrounds.

At the other end of the scenic scale was Beckton gasworks in Essex, one of the largest plants of its kind in the world, a dreary honeycomb of black coal stacks, tar plants and myriad pipes festooning the buildings – with an all-

ABOVE *No. 3 on the Bass Railway waits at an ornate bracket signal.*

RIGHT *Two of the Beckton gasworks locomotives. With no cabs because of restricted headroom, the drivers were exposed to all weathers.*

pervading smell of gas. In these Stygian surroundings the little locomotives, brightly painted and highly polished, were a positive delight to see as they scurried about their duties between coal heaps and retort houses. There were over fifty of them, a very mixed fleet with some dating from the 1870s.

When the National Coal Board was formed in 1947 they wisely refrained from imposing a standard livery for their locomotives, but left the choice to the Area Boards. Blue with yellow lining was selected for most new engines, but in many cases the old company colours were perpetuated – green, deep red, black, all with various linings. So there was plenty to interest the enthusiast and to please the photographer in the days when colour photography was becoming increasingly popular.

The early industrial locomotive photographers were content to record the engines alone, to the neglect of their working background – which in many cases could hardly be regarded as aesthetically pleasing. This omission was put right as time went on and people began to realise that industrial processes – though often dirty and laborious – were worthy of recording in their own right. The locomotive was shown not as a piece of equipment to be admired but as a unit carrying out a job of work. In iron- and steelworks, for example, locomotives were involved in the whole process: they brought in truckloads of iron ore, moved ladles of molten metal, tipped slag, shifted bars of iron to the rolling mills, and eventually put the finished products on to the main-line siding for collection.

Away from the smoke and turmoil of the factories, the railways of rural industries usually offered a much simpler picture, and in more agreeable surroundings, so there was a natural tendency for cameramen to concentrate on these more photogenic locations. It was in the rural areas, too, that most of the narrow-gauge railways were to be found. The slate and granite quarries of north Wales were served almost entirely by narrow-gauge tramways and were a favourite haunt of enthusiasts.

As you travelled up the valley to Llanberis, plumes of steam could be seen dotted over the mountainside. Then followed the laborious climb up cable-worked inclines and along mountain ledges to see tiny engines (mostly without any cabs) hard at work taking slate to the mill or waste to the tip. The scene was ready-made for the photographer; all you needed were good lungs and legs, and a bit of luck in finding a day when it wasn't raining, and the slopes were not shrouded in mist.

ABOVE *Another variant of the crane tank idea could be found at the Stanton steelworks of Stanton and Staveley Ltd.*

TOP RIGHT *Working at an altitude of 1600 feet in the Welsh mountains created a hardy breed of enginemen. This is 'Irish Mail' with her crew at Dinorwic.*

Stone quarries in England offered the opportunity of seeing narrow-gauge activity in less demanding if less spectacular scenery. There were the granite quarries of Devon and Leicestershire, the marvellous series of chalk quarries in Kent, and – perhaps best known – the ironstone quarries of the east Midlands.

If Ivo Peters were asked to name his favourite industrial railways he would almost certainly choose those serving the ironstone quarries. They have been my favourite, too, for over fifty years, and we are not alone. When prints from the collection of a well-known photographer of industrials were made available, the demand for photographs of the ironstone quarries exceeded by far those of any other industry. It is not that there is a cult, but just that these lines offered all the special attractions of industrial railways in the pleasantest of surroundings: the freshness of the open air; the contrast of green fields and red ore, black smoke and white steam; the great variety from one tramway to another only a few miles away; interesting engineering features; and ancient locomotives working alongside modern ones.

The happy circumstance by which the colourful job of extracting iron-stone was divorced from the grubbier process of converting the ore into iron and steel is rooted in industrial history. The ironmasters of the early nineteenth century were on the lookout for sources of iron to replace their rapidly dwindling reserves of high-grade ores such as haematite; the Jurassic ores, occurring in a wide band across the Midlands from Lincolnshire to Wiltshire, provided the answer. Development was entirely conditional on the railway network of the time; beds of ore close to the surface and near a railway were opened up first, and more distant workings in later years – the bulk of the output going to ironworks outside the district. The ironstone beds were on average only about 10ft thick, hence quarries tended to be wide rather than deep. In the 1930s when enthusiast photography began, the quarries still working were further from the main-line railways, as the ore closer to them had been exhausted. The tramways were thus longer and more interesting.

There were some very old quarries that had somehow survived the ups and downs of the iron industry for three-quarters of a century. The one claimed by the owners to be the oldest ironstone quarry in the Midlands was at Brixworth, near Northampton, not far from the famous Saxon church. This quarry dated from 1873, with a 4ft-gauge tramway operated by two locomotives of comparable age. I well remember one autumn day sitting on the parapet of the bridge where the line passed under the road, watching the vintage *Brixworth* No. 1, with its title in yellow lettering on green paintwork and a burnished copper cap to its chimney, ambling down from the pits with a rake of wooden wagons laden with yellow-brown ore rattling along behind. I followed the train to the loco shed – a rather flimsy erection of slatted wood set against the cutting wall – and here the 'rope runner', who combined the duties of fireman and shunter, was busy filling its tank. While this was going on, sister engine *Louisa* came puffing up the bank with a train of empties for the quarry. I was offered, and gladly accepted, a footplate trip.

Louisa had no cab, just a weatherboard, and on wet days the driver had to manage with a tarpaulin. At the quarry working face a small diesel digger was busy loading another lot of wagons and when these were full we coupled up and set off down the line, passing No. 1 as before at the shed. The line to the BR sidings ran downhill, and between the rails were old rollers and pieces of cable. I asked the driver about these but he could not recall their ever having been used to assist haulage. Meanwhile, he was busy with the brakes on the steepest bits. At the sidings we ran round the train and pushed the wagons one at a time to the tipping dock for emptying. Then we were off again to the quarries; uphill this time, with the blast from the chimney fetching down the

RIGHT *With a string of ironstone trucks in tow, Kettering Furnaces No. 6 follows the hedgerow of a Northamptonshire cornfield in high summer.*

autumn leaves in a golden shower from the trees lining the cutting. I said farewell at the summit, little thinking that I should never see this line again. I suppose we all believed these anachronisms would last for ever. My one regret is that I took no photographs. Even Ivo Peters did not see this line, I fear, but he did record another one, owned by a different company, only a mile or so away.

The line Ivo Peters photographed dated back only to 1913 (in time of war or the threat of it, demand for ironstone increased sharply) and had a complicated history. In its final form the transport arrangements included a 3ft-gauge tramway from the pits to a tipping dock where the wooden wagons emptied their loads into wagons for a 2-mile run to the BR sidings in the valley. The narrow-gauge locomotives were much younger than those at Brixworth but no less attractive, and very nicely kept.

Even better known was the 3ft-gauge line at Kettering; in this case the ore was used in furnaces on the spot. It was a gem of a railway with delightful names such as 'Chestnut Tree Loop', 'Glen Cutting' and 'Violet Lane Bridge', evocative of its rural setting. There were two kinds of locomotive, small four-wheelers and larger six-wheelers, but all fully in keeping with the rural scene

as they bobbed and swayed through the cornfields and alongside hedges. In the declining years of operation hardly a day passed without some amateur photographer being on hand to record it.

Further east, in Leicestershire, narrow-gauge railways had been extracting iron ore from the Duke of Rutland's Belvoir estates since the 1880s. One of them, at Eastwell, had a cable-worked incline down to the BR line in the Vale of Belvoir. Such inclines were once commonplace as a means of moving minerals from high ground to railways in the valleys, but they were labour intensive, and Eastwell's was one of the few to survive the Second World War. Trains of thirty loaded steel tubs were brought to the top of the incline by one of the larger engines and then manhandled one at a time and tied to the cable. At the bottom of the hill a lad would take them off the cable, run them to the 'tip' over the BR siding, and reattach them to the cable for the return trip. Working eight hours a day in all weathers, I don't suppose he noticed the beauty of the view.

The tramway was quite a long one at this time – 4 miles or so – threading its way round the village of Eaton. The locomotives were mixed, small ones in the quarries and larger ones for the longer trip to the top of the incline. Inevitably the end came, with a decision to use lorries instead of the railway. On 21 October 1959, the last day of rail operation, Eli Coy, who had presided over the system for many years, attached a bunch of wild marjoram and hawkweed from the tramway cutting to the last wagon, chalked a farewell notice, and away it went. The lorries were efficient, cut costs and were more comfortable for working, but no one pretended they had the attraction of the little railway. Belvoir had lost a graceful addition to its fields.

Away to the south of Wellingborough was the old set of workings grouped round Irchester. To this day 'Roman Town' still has the nicks in the surrounding ramparts where the tramway was taken across the site. Quarrying at Irchester was very different from Kettering: in contrast to Kettering's shallow pits that made little difference to the surface, the stone at Irchester was a long way below ground level and the locomotives (standard-gauge this time) were dwarfed by the high quarry walls. The quarries belonged to a steelworks in the north-east, so the locomotive stock consisted mostly of redundant engines from the works – and a very mixed lot they were. They often arrived in poor condition and were taken into the workshops at Irchester where, with very

OPPOSITE *An early morning scene on the narrow-gauge Scaldwell system.*
Like all the ironstone lines, this railway has now entirely vanished.

primitive equipment, the fitters would turn them into useful engines, sometimes by the process of 'cannibalisation' – pinching bits off one to put on another. As a result there was always a graveyard of old engines with small or large parts missing, and in-service locomotives with oddities in their composition. But they *worked*, and worked hard, for there was a very stiff bank out of the quarry.

When the quarries were closed, one section was designated a Country Park so that visitors can still see the impressive appearance of these workings. Also established here is a group of enthusiasts dedicated to locomotive preservation. They have made a wonderful job of a 1-metre gauge locomotive from Wellingborough quarries and are now working on others.

In complete contrast to the Irchester set-up, with its motley assembly of rebuilt locomotives, rough track and cavernous quarries, was the Wroxton area of north Oxfordshire with a well-kept fleet, superlative track of near main-

ABOVE *'Nancy', on the 3ft-gauge Eastwell quarry system, was a substantial locomotive, fitted with side tanks rather than the more usual saddle tank.*

TOP RIGHT *On the Oxfordshire Ironstone Railway at Wroxton, 'Basic' crosses the Wroxton to Hanwell road, passing Ivo Peters' faithful Mk VI Bentley, in which he clocked up 250 000 miles, mostly in pursuit of trains!*

line standard, and workings mostly less than 20ft deep. Whilst Irchester had been going since the 1870s, Wroxton was a product of the First World War. 'Hornton Stone' was nationally known as a building material and today is still quarried for decorative purposes. That so large an area of easily-accessible ironstone had not been worked before was due solely to its distance from any railway. But under the spur of wartime necessity, and with Government backing, a group of companies got together to open the area by laying a 4-mile railway from Wroxton to the Great Western Railway near Banbury, with German prisoners-of-war helping in the work.

In the 1920s and 1930s demand fell short of potential, but as the Second World War loomed output was stepped up continually, quarry lines were extended, more locomotives were purchased and the 'main line' was doubled. The latter boasted features uncommon on industrial railways – signals and quarter-mile posts, for example. The locomotives, except for a few obtained secondhand, were painted crimson lake with red and yellow lining. They were maintained in tiptop condition by Bill Rogers, a 'steam man' who was always willing to help visiting enthusiasts.

There were two sets of locomotives – six-wheelers for working between Wroxton and Banbury, and four-wheelers in the quarries; and it became the custom to give them boys' and girls' names respectively. Some of the earlier engines had names associated with the history of the area: *The Dean* and *The Bursar* referred to officers in the Oxford colleges who leased the land, while *Lord North* and *Sir Thomas* were former owners of Wroxton Abbey. Traffic was intensive and the management was willing to allow visits and photography; and at the end of the day you could ride back on the 'workmen's train', an ex-GWR brake van.

Today ironstone quarrying at Wroxton is only a memory. The former railway cutting above the locomotive sheds is a footway between housing estates; that at Friars Hill, Wroxton, is a nature reserve. The former offices and other buildings are occupied by an engineering firm, and if you ask they may give you permission to browse round. You can peer into the long locomotive shed, still with track in the floor, and think of the times it held engines sizzling after the day's work. The quarries have been returned to agriculture and there has been no great devastation of the countryside. There were two bridges under the Stratford road where branches to quarries passed through, and in contrast to the utilitarian bridges usual in such circumstances, these were beautifully made. They remain for farm access, and from the parapets the former railway trackbed can often be picked out by crop marks.

Industrial railways hold endless fascinations for the enthusiast: the rich variety in track gauge, motive power and operating methods, often to be found in a small area; and the ever-present element of discovery. The day-to-day routine of these little railways probably did not alter much, but the visitor could feel that there was always the chance of something fresh – a different locomotive at work, perhaps even a new one on its first run. Until recent years there was no published information available on these railways – it had to be obtained at first hand, and there was always the possibility of discovering a hitherto unrecorded location.

A large number and wide variety of industrial locomotives found their way to railway preservation centres, where in fact they considerably outnumber main-line locomotives since, being smaller, they were cheaper to buy and to run. At some of the sites – the Bowes Railway, Tyne and Wear; the Pontypool and Blaenafon Railway, Gwent; the Scottish Industrial Railway Centre, Dalmellington, for example – these locomotives regularly run passenger trains.

As for industrial railways that have been closed, tracing them can be a fascinating exercise, but not always an easy one. In built-up areas the ground will almost certainly have been put to other use, while in country districts a lot will depend on the demands of agriculture. Let us take a couple of extreme examples. On the 20-mile Wissington Railway in Norfolk, over which beet was taken to the sugar factory for processing, the track was at ground level and often almost invisible. When it was lifted the fen simply took over again. On the other side of Britain, the 7-mile Croesor Tramway carried slates from near Blaenau Ffestiniog to Porthmadog, paralleling the famous Festiniog Railway; but it is over 50 years since slates went this way and the rails have long been lifted. In this remote valley there was no call for restoration, nor did natural vegetation make much headway, so it is still possible to follow the trackbed and take a look at the relics of Victorian engineering in the breath-taking inclines from the quarries high up in the mountains. I walked the tramway two years ago and was rewarded with a superb day, the peaks sharply etched against a blue sky. It gave me a sense of exhilaration to gaze down the sunlit valley with the trackbed stretching towards the distant sea; while the walk back provided a marvellous panorama of Snowdonia.

There are certainly more people than ever interested in industrial railways. They record those still in use today, trace those that have ceased to exist, delve into archives and search out old employees for their information.

But the once-familiar steam-worked industrial railway is now a thing of the past in Britain, and we must be grateful for the films and photographs of Ivo Peters and others, and the writings of people who made it their task to capture for us the atmosphere of these railways. So may I end with an appeal? If *you* come across old photographs or snippets of information, please pass them on to your local Record Office or to an interested enthusiast if you know one, so that they may be kept for posterity. So many times in the past I have heard of unique photographs being thrown away simply because they were thought to be of no interest – *but they are.*

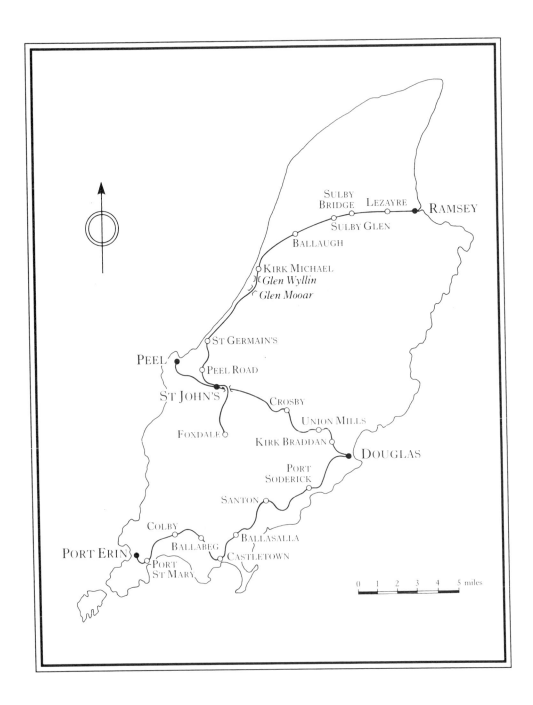

SULBY
BRIDGE   LEZAYRE   RAMSEY
SULBY GLEN
BALLAUGH

KIRK MICHAEL
Glen Wyllin
Glen Mooar

St Germain's

PEEL
Peel Road
St John's   CROSBY
UNION MILLS
FOXDALE   KIRK BRADDAN
DOUGLAS
PORT
SODERICK
SANTON
COLBY
BALLABEG   BALLASALLA
PORT ERIN   CASTLETOWN
PORT
St MARY

0 1 2 3 4   5 miles

THE
ISLE OF MAN
RAILWAY

—○4○—

DAVID ROWLANDS

On a shelf just out of reach of my sticky, child's fingers was a line of drab, dull-looking volumes comprising my father's collection of railway books: meagre enough in those immediate post-Second World War years. They were out of reach because I had already attempted to augment the illustrations with my coloured crayons. One of those books was Ian Macnab's *History and Description of the Isle of Man Railway*; but it was to be some years before I was allowed to take it down and discover what a mine of information it was. Meantime the magazine pile was closer to hand and, from among a jumble of ancient issues, I chanced on the December 1942 *Model Railway News*, with photographs and an article by John H. Ahern on his model of one of the pretty little Isle of Man tank locomotives, which he christened *Manx Kitten*. I kept that issue for many years, delighting in Jack Ahern's photos, and indeed I still have it. Macnab and Ahern between them first introduced me to the railways of the Isle of Man, which have been an interest ever since.

The 3ft-gauge railways began in the Isle of Man as a development from the 2ft-gauge light/mineral railway movement which started in Wales with Charles Spooner and the Festiniog. To most people 'narrow gauge' meant Wales and slate, the Lynton and Barnstaple, the Leek and Manifold and suchlike; all 2ft- and 2ft 6ins-gauges. There was something positively *foreign* about 3ft-gauge. It conjured up images of a mist-girt home of wizardry and magic – every mainlander's view of the Isle of Man. And indeed, as befitted an island kingdom with parliament, people, cats, language, money and customs of its own, there were many features which made construction and operation of the Isle of Man railways unique in the British Isles.

From the capital of Douglas, the Isle of Man Company pushed its rails across the central valley to Peel with no major problems other than the rather marshy and restricted site at Peel itself, and the need to draft in Irish and Welsh labour when the Manxmen followed their ancient seasonal pastimes of fishing and smuggling. The Douglas to Peel section opened in 1873, and from the start was operated by the pretty little tank locomotives built by Beyer Peacock. They looked well in their green livery (though I personally prefer the Indian red of 1944–67), copper-capped chimneys with brass running numbers on each side of the stack, and polished bell-mouthed domes with Salter's balance springs very much in evidence. Inclined cylinders and sloping smokebox front were to become recognisable trademarks of Beyer Peacock.

These first engines proved so successful that the type was adhered to throughout the years. The first series of engines (Nos. 1–9) served well, but growth of traffic and heavier carriages required an enlarged design after 1905,

ABOVE *Douglas shed in June 1968, with the unique Manx Northern Railway locomotive 'Caledonia' on the left. The wheels were from coaches whose bodies had been mounted in pairs on new bogie underframes.*

TOP RIGHT *Crosby Station on the Peel line in June 1961. No. 11 'Maitland' runs in from Douglas with a children's picnic special to Kirk Michael.*

when Nos. 10–13 were supplied. (No. 14 was identical with Nos. 1–9.) The new design was so successful that Nos. 4–6 were rebuilt with larger boilers.

No. 15, *Caledonia*, was the odd one out: an 0–6–0 type built by Dübs and Co. Although very powerful, she was large and heavy and damaged the track, so that she was little used in latter days except for snow clearance. The final enlargement of the Island type came with No. 16, *Mannin*, in 1926. She was quite popular with the drivers, but less so with fitters since her bulk gave much reduced access to working parts.

The Company's second route, from Douglas to Port Erin, presented rather more difficult terrain than the Peel line, necessitating an almost continuous climb to the cliffs at Port Soderick, a descent inland to Santon, and a coastal route to Castletown. Trains in both directions needed banking when they were carrying a heavy load of passengers. From Castletown, the final section was fairly level to Port Erin. The Douglas to Port Erin line opened in 1874 and survives today. Its centenary was marked with special trains. The centenary for the Railway had come in 1973, but the earlier closure of the original (Peel) line made celebrations inappropriate.

The Isle of Man Company held back on its proposal to build a line north to Ramsey, and eventually it was a different company, the Manx Northern, who opened this line in 1879. Scenically it was the finest, but it was also the most costly, involving a series of rock cuttings and ledges along the western coastline, and construction of viaducts across the glens Mooar and Wyllin which run down to the northern plains from Snaefell and Barrule. Although not primarily built for freight, the sprawling terminus at Ramsey with its attractive stone buildings handled large quantities of imported goods for inland distribution. The stone station buildings were a feature of this northern line

ABOVE *The rural charm of the Manx railway system is captured by Ivo Peters as the 11.45 for Port Erin climbs away from Douglas on 3 July 1963.*
RIGHT *No. 12 'Hutchinson' runs along the west coast in July 1963.*

which set it apart from the others. The Ramsey line left the Douglas–Peel section at St John's, as did the Foxdale branch, a little-used line, intended primarily for transporting minerals, which opened in 1883, and eventually bankrupted the Manx Northern who had rashly undertaken to operate it.

The original passenger coaches were small four-wheelers, each with three partitioned compartments. Bogie coaches and electric lighting were introduced by the turn of the century, well ahead of many UK main-line railways. Many of the four-wheel coaches were converted to bogie stock by joining pairs end to end, and the surplus wheels could be seen in Douglas yard for many years. Few of the intermediate stations had platforms, so the coaches had two running boards to assist passengers in alighting. Two diesel railcars were acquired from the County Donegal railway in 1961 and were run back to back – they were the first 'new' stock since the 1920s. The flamboyant red and cream livery of the coaches – particularly striking when clean – gave a fresh look to the trains no matter how much the older vehicles sagged, or how tired the staff, engines and system might actually be.

The railway was intended to tap the huge and increasing tourist traffic arriving by steamer, for in the summer the island became a vast holiday camp. Stations and facilities were designed for the handling of large crowds, with wide platforms to accommodate maybe 1000 or more passengers from a single train. At the peak of prosperity in the 1920s, the railway carried some 1.6 million to 1.8 million people annually. For a while the railway companies managed to hold off the incursion of road transport by buying out the rival bus companies and operating an integrated system. This was also the period of 'Go-As-You-Please' tickets giving unlimited bus and train travel on the island for periods of two, three, four or seven days.

So, unlike other 'preserved' lines where tourist traffic has displaced the original purpose of the railway, visitors who travel on the Isle of Man Railway today actually continue the tradition.

ABOVE *Early morning activity at Douglas on 27 June 1961 with (left to right) Nos. 13 'Kissack', 11 'Maitland', and 12 'Hutchinson' on a train for Port Erin.*
TOP RIGHT *Tywyn Station on the Talyllyn with No. 6 'Douglas' on a train to Abergynolwyn in 1963.*

M_y early enthusiasm for narrow-gauge railways continued, and in 1953, still of prep-school age, I found myself unofficially attached to a volunteer working party digging out drainage ditches for the Talyllyn Railway at Tywyn: an early lesson in the unromantic aspects of railway operation. Easily bored, I made a nuisance of myself by getting soaking wet. To keep me out of further mischief while I dried off, I was given a year-old copy of *Trains Illustrated* magazine.

There I found an article on the 3ft-gauge Tralee and Dingle which really fired my enthusiasm, though I did not properly register that the line was only surviving by the merest thread – the once-monthly cattle train. I wrote to a cousin in Dublin (believing it to be close to Tralee) asking him to 'pop down' and take some photographs for me. By the time he got there with his box camera in July 1953, the Dingle had closed for ever, and a few snaps of derelict stock in Tralee yard were all I got for his trouble.

During the 1960s, I was one of the many who despaired and hid their heads as branch and cross-country lines of British Railways were axed with no regard for their place in the community, and steam was being phased out. But while some of us were inactive, a number of far-sighted enthusiasts were capturing on film what was left of this vanishing heritage.

Two incidents brought narrow-gauge railways back into my life. First, my fiancée gave me a copy of Pat Whitehouse's book *On the Narrow Gauge* (1964). Mr Whitehouse is widely known today as a founding father of the preservation movement because of his involvement with the Talyllyn and the purchase of GWR locomotives No. 4555 and *Clun Castle*. Two decades back, he was perhaps better known for the BBC TV *Railway Roundabout* programmes, for his interest in the Irish narrow gauge and particularly for his definitive book on the Tralee and Dingle Railway.

On the Narrow Gauge is a most enjoyable book, presenting a capsule history of narrow gauge in the British Isles, with lively essays evoking the spirit and atmosphere of the vanished workaday lines. Most important to me, however, were the sections which dealt with the birth of the 3ft-gauge in the Isle of Man, and the vivid account of the once-monthly train to Dingle Fair. My former interest in the Tralee and Dingle was reawakened, stimulated by the Ivo Peters photographs that Whitehouse had included.

The name Ivo Peters was familiar to me only from scenes of his O-gauge model railway in the *Bassett Lowke Model Railway Handbook*, many photographs in *Trains Illustrated*, and an occasional article in the *Railway Magazine* on the Somerset & Dorset. He and Pat Whitehouse seemed very grand people, whom I should not dare to approach.

The second incident arose unexpectedly through my work. The Ministry of Agriculture gave me, in 1970, a colleague and a room-mate who, on that million-to-one chance, was a narrow-gauge enthusiast with a particular love of the Isle of Man and Irish lines. A few days after I first met Dave Pinniger, he handed me the journal of the Narrow Gauge Society. The cover ... well, on the cover was quite the finest narrow-gauge picture I have ever seen! Captured by Ivo Peters on 29 June 1951, it showed locomotives Nos. 1T and 2T arriving at Dingle. Throwing reserve to the winds, I sat down that night and wrote to Ivo Peters, care of the *Railway Magazine*.

As it happened, Ivo was ill in hospital at the time my letter was delivered, and it is entirely typical of his courtesy and kindness that, despite this, he took the trouble to reply within a couple of days. 'The Dingle' forged an immediate

TOP RIGHT *The once-a-month service on the Tralee and Dingle reaches its destination at Dingle on 29 June 1951, in Ivo Peters' inspirational photograph.*

bond between us, and he invited Dave Pinniger and me to visit him in Bath.

We parked by chance in the then ghostly shell of Green Park station and walked uphill to Ivo's house in Royal Crescent, announcing ourselves on the doorbell with the signalman's bell-code for 'train on line'. How many hundreds of visitors: ex-Somerset & Dorset railwaymen, clergy, engineers, tv producers, publishers, cooks, bottle-washers and company directors must have done the same, and shared the warm welcome we were given.

Many people have wondered how it was that Ivo always managed to obtain such whole-hearted co-operation for his filming from railway management and staff. Two minutes of his company would suffice to answer that question; and it is typified by a story he often told about his first visit to the Isle of Man, which bears re-telling here in his own words:

One evening in January 1961, a friend of mine who held a senior executive position in British Railways came to dinner and to see my 1960 'crop' of 16mm films. When the viewing was over, he said, 'And where are you planning to go this summer?' To which I replied that I longed to film the Isle of Man Railway, but I gathered that, unlike British Railways, they did not grant photographic permits. 'Oh', said my BR friend, 'I don't think that should present much of a problem. I will get our PRO to contact Mr Bond, Head of the Isle of Man Tourist Board. I am sure we can get things fixed up for you.'

And so it came about that one morning in June 1961, accompanied by my friend Norman Lockett, I set sail from Liverpool for Douglas in the Isle of Man, where I was to call on Mr Bond who would introduce me to Mr Sheard, general manager of the IOMR. Mr Bond gave us a very warm welcome and promptly took us round to the headquarters of the railway, where we were told that Mr Sheard was not yet back from lunch. However, Mr Sheard's assistant appeared on the scene asking if he could help, and when Mr Bond explained the purpose of our visit, the immediate reply was, 'Oh, that's impossible. Mr Sheard *never* grants permission for *any* photography.' My heart sank!

It was a glorious, hot summer's afternoon and so, whilst waiting for the return of Mr Sheard, we all adjourned to a bar in the station forecourt to refresh ourselves. However, no sooner had we sat down than an elderly, distinguished-looking gentleman passed by the open doorway. 'Mr Sheard!' called out our IOMR friend, and, jumping to his feet, he ushered in the general manager of the Isle of Man Railway. As soon as he was comfortably seated, and armed with a glass of light ale, Mr Sheard turned towards Mr Bond and said, 'And what is the purpose of this meeting?' Mr Bond answered, 'Mr Peters, and his friend Mr Lockett, are over from the mainland and would much appreciate it if you would allow them to photograph the railway.' There was a short pause, then came the sharp reply, 'Oh no, quite out of the question. I never allow photography' – and then, turning suddenly to his assistant, barked, 'Do I?' 'No, sir,' came the instant reply, 'that's what I told them sir.' 'But', interjected Mr Bond, 'these gentlemen are recommended by British Railways.' I thought Mr Sheard was going to do himself an injury! Purple in the face, he suddenly exploded, 'This is *not* British Railways. This is the Isle of Man Railway of which I am general manager.' His clenched fist came down on the table with a tremendous bang. All five glasses took off vertically to a height of at least half an inch, before crash-landing back on to the marble-topped table. 'Permission refused!' Another tremendous bang on the table, and another instant take-off by the glasses.

The silence which followed seemed interminable. I stared glumly at the floor, thinking what an awful long way I had come for apparently nothing. Then Mr Sheard spoke sharply to his assistant. 'Well, haven't you got any work to do?' Exit in a hurry the assistant. Mr Bond also rose to his feet, saying he had another appointment, and bade us farewell; we were left alone with the still simmering Mr Sheard. We finished our drinks and I asked Mr Sheard if he would like another half pint – but the answer was no, so I got Norman Lockett's and my glasses replenished, thinking that at least we might try and drown our sorrows a little. Then I turned to Mr Sheard and said, 'It is our first visit to the Island; are you sure you won't join us?' – and somewhat to my surprise, this produced the response, 'Well, just a half then.'

Outside the sunshine streamed down in the forecourt, and in the distance we could hear faintly the whistling of the little engines as they went about their duties. Misery surrounded me! Then, half way through his second drink, Mr Sheard suddenly put down his glass and said, 'What exactly was it that you wanted to do, Mr Peters?' I explained how I had hoped to film his line. There was a long pause, then Mr Sheard stood up. 'Well, I don't see why that shouldn't be arranged. Come with me!'

From that moment on, Mr Sheard could not do enough for us. We were introduced to Mr Shaw the locomotive superintendent, the station foreman, and other members of the staff. To all, Mr Sheard said, 'These are two of my friends over from the mainland. They have come to film the Railway. Please give them every assistance and co-operation.'

All I need add is that the next few days were some of the happiest and most successful narrow-gauge filming sessions I ever had.

It never seems to occur to Ivo (who is a very modest fellow indeed) that there is a very simple explanation of Mr Sheard's sudden and completely unexpected change of heart ... and that is the personality of Ivo himself.

On that first visit to Royal Crescent we did a lot of talking and I spent some considerable time with my nose buried in the 1950 and 1951 photograph albums (Ivo's visits to Tralee), but we also had a film before lunch. On subsequent visits Ivo would give us 'The Menu' (a small black notebook listing all his cine films), even though he knew that the Manx films were obligatory so far as we were concerned. 'I took up cine photography too late for the Irish Narrow Gauge,' he said, 'but, you know, I found the Isle of Man Railway even more delightful.'

So the projector was set up, the room was darkened, and we settled down for what was to be the treat of a lifetime.

Genius has been defined as having the capacity to take infinite pains, and this certainly applied to Ivo's film-making. Considerable time would be spent in touring the locale, looking for the right spots to set up the cine and still cameras that would capture the setting as well as the railway. He was concerned not just to make a pretty picture – though he often did that of course – but to give the viewer the full flavour of the operation of these rural railways and a good idea of the communities they served.

Each of Ivo's three films condenses a week of filming into a single working day in the life of the Railway. In a total running time of an hour, we could follow operations much as they had been carried out for 90 years. We could pursue trains from Douglas to Peel and to Ramsey, where no lines now run; and get a unique picture of the intensive daily routine at Douglas, as permitted to no other photographer.

There were the engines at the start of a working day, being coaled by basket and serviced, having their tubes swept and smoke boxes emptied, amidst drifting smoke from their shed-mates on nearby lines. The 'station pilot' (usually No. 13, *Kissack*) fussed around adding wagons or bringing extra coaches from the sidings. All this activity culminated in the departure of Port Erin and Peel/Ramsey trains on morning services. The ever-present *Kissack* banked out the heavier trains and also pulled out the stored (i.e. unserviceable) engines from within the shed for Ivo to film, including *Caledonia* (still clad in winter snow ploughs), and *Thornhill*, the only veteran to retain the elegant spring-balance safety valves. The generally clean engines and burnished brass-work glossed over the mechanical defects, of which Mr Sheard and his staff were only too aware.

Finally the returning trains arrived back at Douglas in the evening light, and under the platform canopies hundreds of passengers alighted, some of them breaking into a run. Was there a steamer connection to be made? The

ABOVE

A St Johns–Ramsey train heads north beside the sea. Sadly, this scenic line has now been abandoned.

LEFT

Approaching Port Soderick on the line from Douglas to Port Erin in 1963.

The view from Douglas
signalbox with No. 10
'G. H. Wood' and
No. 5 'Mona' on duty.
The revival of the
green locomotive livery
was one of the changes
during the 'Ailsa era'.

No. 12 'Hutchinson'
waits at Peel with
a train for Douglas.

A Ramsey–Douglas
train near St Johns in
1968 during the brief
period when the Isle of
Man's railways were re-
opened by Lord Ailsa.

A Douglas to Port Erin train leaving Douglas in 1963, behind No. 10 'G. H. Wood'.

ABOVE
A Barclay saddle tank braves the snow at Cairnhill colliery, Ayrshire.

RIGHT
Two colliery saddle tanks struggle with a heavy load at the Laight dump in Ayrshire.

RIGHT
*The perfect
combination: steam in
a brewery! Bass No. 2
adds a little colour
to the industrial
landscape of Burton-
on-Trent in April 1958.*

BELOW LEFT
*The classic industrial
railway scene on the
Oxfordshire ironstone
system at Wroxton.
'Barabel' waits for
her train to be
loaded in 1964.*

BELOW *Although built as late as 1938, 'Wissington'
looks every inch the Victorian industrial engine.*

The Southern's arch rival, the GWR, produced traditional locomotives with brass and copper fittings. The 'County' class were the last of the line.

A London-bound express leaves Honiton Tunnel on the Exeter– Waterloo main line in 1964.

The 11.48 from Plymouth leaves Seaton Junction for Waterloo in 1964 behind 'Battle of Britain' class Pacific 'Sir Archibald Sinclair'.

*Axminster change for Lyme Regis.
'Merchant Navy' class Pacific
No. 35019 passes No. 30584 on the
branch line train.*

*Vintage steam at Lyme
Regis in July 1960.
This classic Victorian
locomotive now works
on the Bluebell
Railway in Sussex.*

*Many elderly tank
engines survived on
the Southern branch
lines. Here M7 class
No. 30670 heads for
Exeter with the milk
train from Crediton
in July 1961.*

drivers lost no time in uncoupling their engines from the trains, and then began the evening game of putting away coaches into the carriage sidings. Why they did this, instead of leaving the assembled trains under the sheltering platform canopies, is a mystery; but it happened every night, before the engines were bedded down. Each film ends with engines – their fires dropped – moving into the sheds on their last gasps of steam.

A number of vivid impressions remain with me from seeing Ivo's films: the startling colours of the red and cream trains in the lush green landscape, and how particularly attractive the Indian red livery of the engines looked in sunlight. The red and cream name-boards nestle amidst the encompassing foliage of the stations. The trains leave Douglas past the splendid gantry signal with its twin arms for the two separate main lines (Peel/Ramsey and Port Erin), with clouds of steam vigorously pulsating from the open cylinder drain-cocks – often alleged by frustrated snapshot photographers to be at the instigation of the forbidding Mr Sheard to ruin their pictures by enveloping the departures in steam! Ivo's films show this Manx trait to perfection, including one train which actually moves off, presumably on the guard's wave, before the station signal has dropped to 'Clear'.

ABOVE *The substantial and extensive station at Douglas in 1961 with the platform canopies (now demolished) and goods yard (now torn up).*

Most of all, though, I carry images of tiny trains silhouetted against the skyline or seascape in crossing the two elegant viaducts or running along the grassy embankments. In one of these sequences, the train leaves a lovely woolly streamer of smoke and steam above and trailing behind the coaches. The films also show the decrepit track and how the speeding trains rocked and rolled on some sections.

One peculiarity of the Isle of Man Railway was the ballasting of track up to rail height, so that the sleepers were all but invisible. The ballast often had a distinctive odour, due to the use of gasworks waste as a weed-killer.

Because of Mr Sheard's restrictive policy about photographic permits, there is very little film of the Isle of Man Railway from the 1930s to the 1960s. Ivo's 1961 and 1963 films now provide a rare and comprehensive coverage, depicting the line much as it had been for decades and with many of its unique practices still in evidence: the slotted signals where the semaphore arm vanished into the post; the distinctive whistle signals given by train crews.

TOP LEFT *The view from Douglas signal box on 28 June 1961. No. 12 'Hutchinson' brings in the 4.15 from Port Erin. A fence now divides the site, cutting off the signal box from what remains of the railway.*

LEFT *No. 5 'Mona' and No. 14 'Thornhill' inside Douglas shed. Both locomotives are now over 100 years old.*

ABOVE *The 1.45 Ramsey–Douglas train, behind No. 8 'Fenella', crosses the lattice-girder viaduct at Glen Mooar in June 1961.*

Cleaned and polished engines were festooned with tins, jugs or cans of oil, their canvas weather curtains sometimes hiding drivers in cloth caps (not grease-tops) stealing a quiet puff or two, since smoking on the footplate was forbidden. The little engines were decidedly nippy, and trains often reached 40–45mph, very high speeds for narrow-gauge operation. The engines were coaled up by basket, and the orderly, walled stacks of coal at Douglas can be seen in Ivo's films. Then there were the hand signals given between station staff, guards and train crews, and the use of white flags (rather than red or green) at crossings; and the often simultaneous departure from St John's of Peel and Ramsey trains (frowned on by management; indeed the timetable purposely separated them by two minutes) in an apparent race which never failed to delight passengers and observers, though the gradients made it a foregone conclusion. Palm trees and tropical plants grew on the station plat-forms – a rare sight to British eyes except in southern Devon and Cornwall. Lush foliage and flowering shrubs sheltered intermediate stations, and Ivo was particularly taken with the beauty of Union Mills – a beauty not reflected in the name – and the ivy-covered buildings at Port Soderick.

ABOVE *No. 12 'Hutchinson' shunting at St John's, where the Ramsey and Peel lines diverged.*

Wartime internees and POWs must have had a much less romantic view of the railway which served their camps and thus earned welcome wartime revenue. The German archaeologist Gerhard Bersu and his wife Mary were out of favour with the Nazis and had been excavating in Britain in 1939 when war broke out. They were interned for the duration at Port Erin and the camp authorities were persuaded to allow a programme of excavations from 1941–46, led by Bersu and staffed by camp volunteers with armed guards. These excavations provided valuable archaeological information on Manx history, and it is interesting to picture the trains carrying internees and their guards to the sites near Castletown. Visiting Manx Museum authorities, there to assess progress, would quietly drop tins of his favourite snuff into Bersu's wellingtons.

The decline of freight on the IOMR did not set in until the 1950s. Cattle traffic dwindled away to road haulage, but vans of soap powder still went regularly from Douglas, and fish (usually kippers from the factory at Peel) from the ports. Throughout the early 1960s the valiant Mr Sheard kept his ageing railway operating, despite declining passenger receipts, lack of track maintenance and boiler renewals for the engines. The difficulties of this task should not be underestimated, for although the IOMR was nominally self-contained and sufficient, many of the works facilities were extremely primitive and tedious. There was no welding equipment at Douglas, for example: drilling and rivetting were a necessity.

The package holiday boom, luring away traditional visitors to the Costa del Sol, hit hard at tourist receipts in the 1960s; for, truth to tell, the island was becoming less appealing to a younger generation of money spenders with more leisure time. Nor was the tedious and often uncomfortable sea-crossing any inducement to visit. As well as discouraging tourism, this problem of access was also to hinder the supply of volunteer labour for the IOMR in later years – a problem that has become critical in recent times.

In the spring of 1965 Mr Sheard died, and at the end of the season, heavy operating losses had been incurred. It was the end of an era.

The unprecedented stoppage of all traffic 'for urgent track repairs' from the autumn of 1965 lasted until 1967, when, amidst much debate, the Marquess of Ailsa took out a 21-year lease (with the option to cease at five years) and resumed operations. Ivo's third film covers this period, when he visited the line with the late Rev. Teddy Boston, a railway enthusiast who took a leading role in the reopening ceremonies by driving a flag-bedecked and repainted *Caledonia* through the tape across the rails.

It is a difficult era to appraise with detachment, for much that was of value (notably some historic coaches) were scrapped, destroyed or just vanished; but at first trains were kept running on all three lines and two engines were reboilered. An ambitious timetable and return to Sunday working, plus a number of imaginative traffic moves (travel and lunch tickets for example), threw great strain on the staff, however, and industrial relations were not of the best. According to one apocryphal tale often told of this period, a driver was heard to say, 'I can empty the engine's drain cocks, but I dun't have time for a pee myself.'

The 'Ailsa era' was marked by great enthusiasm from the promoters, as typified by the repainting of locomotives in the original green livery, which partly quelled criticism of operating practices (two trains collided at Union Mills, fortunately without serious injury to passengers), lack of long-term maintenance, and damage to railway property; but harsh economic realities forced closure of the Peel and Ramsey lines in 1968, and a Manx government subsidy was given from 1969. The very difficulty of access to the island that had preserved the uniqueness of the line now prevented much help from outside volunteer labour as was common with such struggling or preserved concerns on the mainland. From 1969, Ailsa's agents operated the Port Erin line only (in a 'Victorian Steam Railway' guise); but Ailsa took advantage of the five-year clause to withdraw from operation in 1972.

Until 1977 the Railway received Manx government subsidy to continue a truncated operation with just one engine and a few coaches – working between Port Erin and Castletown in 1975, extended to Ballasalla in 1976. This was mainly a joy-ride, in association with the newly established Railway Museum in the old bus garage at Port Erin, while attempts were made to sell off the railway site at Douglas. The Railway Company acted decisively in restoring services to Douglas in 1977, following Manx government agreement (and subsidy) late in 1976 for necessary maintenance and improvement work.

In 1977 the Manx government nationalised the railway and a new chapter in the line's history was begun under the management of the Manx Electric Railway Board. With a gradual investment in maintenance and refurbishment, this has resulted in the present-day operation of the south line from a much reduced terminus at Douglas. Sadly it began rather badly with unnecessary demolition of Colby station and removal of the attractive platform awnings at

TOP RIGHT *A heavy train leaves Douglas for Port Erin behind No. 12 'Hutchinson' with much-needed banking assistance in the rear.*

Douglas, leaving passengers without shelter of any sort. Added piquancy and acrimony were given to this era by the existence of two preservation and support groups; and there was understandable confusion among the islanders over whose heads their salvoes were fired.

One of these groups, based in England, has continued its support of the Railway – indeed its intervention at timely moments has saved many artefacts, including Santon station, from demolition. This group is also supportive of the Manx Electric Railway and other systems.

The island is not only a race track and a holiday camp in season, but is itself a Victorian transport museum with its workaday horse trams, the Manx Electric system, steam railway, Snaefell Mountain Railway and (recently restored to working order) the charming little Groudle Glen 2ft-gauge railway. This last has recently occupied the efforts of the other original support and preservation group, who had also played a key role in publicising bad policies in the early days of the steam railway nationalisation.

The annual May 'Transport Weekend' jointly arranged by the Railway and the Isle of Man Railway Society is always a popular event and many of the working exhibits now stored in the Museum are given an outing. Sadly, the disruption and difficulties of the sea services to the island since 1985 have made tourist travel even less straightforward. Air travel is expensive, and mainly used by business visitors and residents. Sea visitors have decreased by 30 per cent since 1983, which means fewer travellers on the Railway and a greater struggle to make ends meet.

No one can afford to be complacent about continued government support for the railway system. Some in the Manx Parliament believe that the Railway should close; and a variety of inappropriate schemes have been proposed. One very real threat to Douglas station is a proposal to build a Post Office complex, sited on a concrete raft above the existing platforms, effectively turning it into an 'underground' station – a most unattractive and smoke-filled prospect for the passengers. Another scheme would see the railway workshops and carriage sheds moved from Douglas to Port Erin. Much of the decrepit shop machinery would not survive such a move, while empty coaching-stock workings from the wrong end of the line for operating purposes would double costs without adding to the income from fares. A further plan would move the railway terminus to a site outside the town, quite impractical in operational terms.

There are also schemes to 'redevelop' the island transport, which may have dire consequences for the historic value of the Railway. One such is a proposal to re-lay the railway line to Peel, in conjunction with a hotel–leisure complex, and to provide a 'vintage' steam rail journey for package-deal patrons of the complex. All of this sounds marvellous, until you remember that some of the trackbed to Peel is sold off to private owners, and that huge sums of money would be needed to renovate the necessary engines and coaching stock for the extra workings. Unfortunately, a much more likely outcome would be some form of miniature railway, totally inappropriate to the island's heritage and setting. These schemes need careful watching and *public* debate if the character of the Isle of Man transport system is not to be destroyed.

In the meantime, however, a great deal of the railway system has gone. Still, there is much left to be grateful for, particularly in comparison to the despair of the early 1970s. Thankfully we have Ivo's film records of the daily operations of 1961 and 1963 and also of the near-miraculous (if brief) Ailsa management in 1968, at the eleventh hour before the Peel and Ramsey lines closed for ever. These films and photographs constitute a precious legacy.

TOP RIGHT *Ballasalla Station on the surviving line to Port Erin. No. 10 'G. H. Wood'*
lets off steam before starting the 2.15 Douglas–Port Erin train in July 1963.

The lack of any other comprehensive record of this unique railway system makes Ivo's work of incalculable value not just for the train buff or the Manx historian but hopefully for the general public too. He provides the chance to experience what is now lost beyond recall, and proves the need to support and to preserve what little of the former Isle of Man Railway system now remains.

A Fowler 'Crab' of the LMS *heads south into Ayr Station in October* 1965.

RETURN TO SCOTLAND

·5·

PETER HANDFORD

In November 1987, a few work-free days during the annual BR Railcard promotional offer of a ticket to anywhere for £10 provided a welcome opportunity for a long overdue return visit to Scotland from my home in East Anglia. In earlier years I had travelled widely on Scottish railways but had never been further north than Dingwall, so, thankful that the machinations of Dr Beeching and his hatchet men had not, meanwhile, succeeded in closing the line to BR's northernmost railhead, I now chose Wick as my destination.

The man in the booking office was not too surprised to be asked for a bargain return ticket to Wick as, like myself, he is a railway enthusiast, despite having to deal with the intricacies of fares on white days and blue days and frequent black days, during which he has to deal with angry passengers, complaining about late or cancelled trains. He too had been to Wick and Thurso, just for the sake of the journey, and while he wrote out the ticket, he asked me to give his regards to Georgemas Junction.

Rail travel has fascinated me since earliest childhood, when trains regularly transported me to school or to visit relatives. Since then, I have been fortunate enough to travel extensively by train throughout Britain and in many other countries. Even today, when so much of the romance and excitement formerly associated with rail travel has been submerged by plastic utilitarianism, I still consider that by far the most restful and civilised way to travel is by train.

The long journey from East Anglia to Wick provided an excellent opportunity to recall previous journeys to Scotland during the final years of steam working when, with cine and still cameras and a tape recorder, Ivo Peters, the late and much-missed Derek Cross and I recorded the workings of steam locomotives on Scottish lines. Earlier memories included wartime journeys – sometimes excruciatingly uncomfortable but always interesting because the routes and motive power were quite unpredictable. The railways played an essential part in the war effort, from the very beginning when children were evacuated from cities to country areas, and later when the remnants of the BEF, of which I was one, returned from France and were dispersed to all corners of Britain. The efforts made by railwaymen in keeping the railways running, in spite of the many problems and dangers, were extraordinary and greatly to their credit. It is shameful that their devotion to duty and the valuable contribution to the war effort made by the railways was rewarded in later years by increasingly shabby treatment from successive governments.

At one stage during wartime army service I had an opportunity to observe railwaymen at work when I was seconded to the Army Film and Photo Unit as a combat cameraman. My section was destined to land on the Normandy beaches on D-Day and during the weeks of waiting before assembling on the south coast, we were given an assignment to film and photograph the movement of armaments, men and materials by rail, from all parts of the country to various depots and assembly areas.

One morning, having been given my first official footplate pass, I joined the driver and fireman of an LMS Stanier 4–6–0 locomotive to film them at work, heading an army supplies train from Willesden in north London to Northampton. These men had already worked a train from their home shed at Bletchley earlier that morning and had only a short break before taking over the Northampton train. There were frequent delays due to congestion on the line, and as a result the 60-mile journey took seven hours. When I left them at Northampton, the crew had no idea how or when they would get home to Bletchley. Apart from such unpredictable and excessive hours, the railwaymen had to cope with many other problems, such as the rostering of locomotives to work for which they were totally unsuited, calling for endless ingenuity and patience from all concerned.

The war ended, leaving the railways in a hopelessly run-down condition, from which, denied proper investment and support, they have never fully recovered. Under the Transport Act of 1947, the railways and a specified section of the road-haulage industry were nationalised and, with the aim of co-ordinating transport by rail, road and waterway, the British Transport Commission was set up. The euphoria which followed did not, however, last long, and vacillations in policy were numerous. In 1953, a new Transport Act handed most road transport back to private interests, effectively ending earlier hopes for an integrated transport policy. Meanwhile it had already become difficult, in an era of relatively high employment, to attract staff to work on the railways, once one of the country's largest employers. Few young men were inclined to take up employment in locomotive sheds, or as firemen, when easier and more regular hours, at higher rates of pay, were on offer for many much less arduous and responsible jobs. This shortage of recruits for footplate work was given as one of the reasons for the decision to get rid of steam locomotives as soon as possible, whatever the cost.

I could see then that the end of the railways as we knew them was in sight, and I resolved to put my professional skill, as a sound recordist, to use in preserving the fascinating multiplicity of sounds of working steam railways.

Many people can see little point in recording steam engines since, in their opinion, they all sound the same. In fact, even to an untrained and unenthusiastic ear, the difference in the sounds of a GWR and LMS engine, or between the rhythms of a three-cylinder and two-cylinder engine, are immediately obvious, as are the differing tones of whistles.

Sounds play a vital part in railway operations, particularly when steam locomotives were in common use. Engine whistles were invaluable as a means of communication between enginemen, guards and signalmen, and as warning at the approach to stations or to men working on the line. Whistle codes were essential to drivers on trains headed by two engines or assisted at the rear by one or more banking engines. The sounds of a working locomotive were a useful indication of its condition and performance and at night, or in conditions of poor visibility, drivers and firemen learned to determine their whereabouts on familiar journeys by listening to the varying sounds of their engine and train. The whistles of guards, station staff and shunters, acknowledged by whistles from the engine, were an essential aid to safe and efficient working. The ultimate safety device, still used today as an adjunct to the audible warning system in the locomotive cab, is the explosive sound of detonators which are placed on the line in an emergency such as a derailment or collision. These detonators give an unmistakable warning of imminent danger when they are exploded by the pressure of the wheels of another train approaching the affected area. Railway sounds have been used in countless films, often simply as an evocative means of establishing a period or creating atmosphere.

When, just after the war, I started to record railway sounds, the equipment available was complex, unwieldy and extremely expensive. I experimented with more manageable but much cruder equipment in the early 1950s, but the results were not good. Then, early in 1955, when transportable tape-recording equipment of a professional standard at last became affordable, I began a self-imposed labour of love: the recording of the widest possible range of steam locomotives at work. The sight and sounds of steam on the railways had always been, and still were then, an accepted part of everyday life. It was hard to realise that, before long, such evocative sounds might vanish. I was determined to do what I could to preserve them, and to make them available, on records, to the largest possible number of people.

ABOVE *The sounds of the steam age: a deafening departure from Bournemouth Central by 'Merchant Navy' No. 35012 'United States Line'.*

TOP RIGHT *At the end of its working life and leaking steam at several points, J27 No. 65795 blasts its way south with coal empties near Sunderland in June 1967.*

Permission for my recording project had to be obtained from BR management, who were somewhat suspicious at first. Tape-recorders were comparatively rare then and their use was often linked to journalism, which was unfortunate because the papers seemed to be conducting an anti-railway campaign. When understandable suspicions had been overcome and higher management had given their full approval, railwaymen all down the line were unfailingly enthusiastic and helpful. An enormous amount of encouragement, advice and information was also given by many enthusiast authors and photographers, among them Ivo Peters.

I approached my new project in an entirely different manner from my film work. Recordings for films are always made with the object of excluding background noise, so that the required individual sounds can be heard in isolation. Various recordings are then mixed together to create any desired atmospheric effect. What I wanted to do now was quite different: to preserve the sounds of trains and associated railway operations in particular settings, including as many as possible of the surrounding sounds, such as birdsong, so that the listener could, as in the case of radio plays, mentally recreate the scene.

I was determined to avoid intrusive and repetitive commentaries – so the records were provided with extensive record sleeve notes, including technical details, to stimulate the listener's imagination by describing the setting and circumstances of each recording.

Some of my earliest recordings were made on the Somerset & Dorset line, so much loved and so well chronicled and photographed by Ivo Peters. There is some satisfaction that the sights and sounds of that railway, now long since completely destroyed, were preserved, but that can be of little comfort to the many people who, often after years of devoted service, suddenly lost their livelihood as a result of the closure.

I made numerous recordings in Scotland from 1956 onwards. Some of the earliest were at Beattock, where I spent many hours, recording the early morning sleeping-car expresses starting out on the climb to Beattock summit, assisted by banking engines. Numerous freight trains, with a variety of motive power, similarly assisted, provided a medley of evocative sounds as they started out from the yard by day and night. In contrast, I recorded a vintage Caledonian tank engine as it left with the short daily goods train on the (soon to be closed) branch line to Moffat.

ABOVE *The sounds of the countryside are drowned briefly by the passing of a Stanier class 5 on the Docker Viaduct in Westmorland.*

RIGHT *In August 1961 2P No. 40569 pilots No. 34045 'Ottery St Mary' on a northbound express in the Midford Valley on the Somerset and Dorset line.*

I remember one morning a group of men, including the shedmaster, standing in bewilderment as strange, explosive sounds were heard on the line from the south. Eventually a Caledonian o–6–o, apparently running on only one of its cylinders, limped into the station and shuddered to a stop with a northbound freight train. The driver, grinning widely and adding profanities to his fireman's description of the journey, then casually told the shedmaster, 'I think we need another engine.'

Some years later I made a number of recordings on the footplates of banking engines, as they assisted passenger and freight trains on the 10-mile climb from Beattock station to the summit. It was endlessly fascinating to observe the hard work of the footplatemen and their expertise in working in harmony with the unseen crew of the distant engine at the head of a long train. One wonders what became of those men and many like them, when diesel and electric locomotives, needing no such assistance, made them redundant.

I made mid-winter recordings on the steeply graded section of the West Highland line between Craigendoran and Arrochar, over which, apart from the passenger and freight trains to and from Fort William, an elderly but still vigorous North British Railway 0–4–4 tank engine worked a push and pull train of two coaches between Craigendoran and Arrochar several times a day. When heavy snowfalls made it difficult to move equipment about at the lineside and sub-zero temperatures caused the recorder to operate temperamentally, or not at all, I retreated to Craigendoran station where, thanks to the porter's hospitality, I thawed out the equipment in front of a blazing fire. In the intervals between defrosting, recordings were made of the manoeuvres of the push and pull train, which started from Craigendoran station, reversed in the yard and then climbed past on the line towards Arrochar. I also recorded Glasgow-bound trains headed by Gresley 2–6–2 tank engines with their distinctive three-cylinder exhaust beat. Later I recorded engines of the same type at work on the underground section of the Glasgow suburban lines. Above ground, beside the line on Cowlairs bank, some passenger trains assisted by banking engines were recorded one evening, vociferously attacking the 1 in 41 climb from Queen Street station.

As I watched what was beginning to happen to the railways, I was more than ever glad that I had managed to capture the sounds of all those locomotives in Scotland. Branch-line closures became more frequent, often accompanied by much jollification. In 1957 came the withdrawal of passenger services on the line to Watlington from Princes Risborough, where I then lived. A silver band played on the platform at Chinnor and joined members of the parish council to travel to Watlington on the, much longer than usual, last train. At Watlington crates of beer were loaded on to the train and on to the crowded footplate, before the engine moved round to the head of the train and left for the final journey to the accompaniment of a fusillade of detonators which had been placed along the line by the shedmaster from Slough, where the branch line engine was based. At that time few people had any suspicion of the holocaust of closures which was to follow in a few years.

The most serious of the social and economic consequences of the closures were the effects on the railwaymen concerned. All down the line, men who

TOP RIGHT *In the last years of Scottish steam, A3 Pacific No. 60052 'Prince Palatine' waits on shed at Edinburgh.*

had jobs which, though not highly paid, had always been regarded as some of the safest available, were suddenly deprived of their livelihood, often in areas where alternative employment was hard to find. Even if they were lucky enough to be offered alternative railway employment that usually meant moving to some unfamiliar area, far from family and friends. Whole towns were often affected. Railway communities all over Britain were destroyed, and the closure of many of the railway workshops had equally drastic effects.

Nevertheless, and in spite of the disastrous consequences of the ASLEF strike in 1955, the last few years of the 1950s were a time of considerable interest on British railways. Many pre-nationalisation and a fair number of even earlier vintage pre-grouping locomotives were still in regular use, and some main-line steam locomotives attained standards of reliability and speed that had not been known since the late 1930s.

One such performance was provided by a legendary driver, the late Bill Hoole, when he was in charge of the fully loaded 295-ton 'SLS Jubilee' special train, organised by the Stephenson Locomotive Society and headed by the A4 Pacific locomotive *Sir Nigel Gresley*, from King's Cross to Doncaster and back, in May 1959. From start to finish the journey was exhilarating: the speed reached 64mph after the first 5 miles from King's Cross, on mainly rising gradients, and then, between mile-posts 30 and 37, an average speed of more than 94mph was maintained, with a maximum in excess of 100mph. Later, on the long climb to Stoke tunnel, the train accelerated to pass Stoke summit at 82mph. During the even more exciting return journey, from Doncaster, a top speed of almost 112mph was achieved between Little Bytham and Essendine. That maximum could certainly have been higher, but the inspector on the footplate reminded Bill Hoole that he had not been authorised to exceed 110mph; at which point an angry blast on *Sir Nigel Gresley*'s whistle emphasised Bill's frustration.

On that round trip between London and Doncaster a total of 55 miles were covered at an average speed of 90mph and another 25 miles at an average of 100mph. A splendid achievement no doubt, but I have been reliably informed that during the late 1950s some extraordinarily high average and maximum speeds were often, though unofficially, attained by enthusiastic footplate crews with trains in normal service on the east coast main line.

I recorded most of the journey on the SLS special train, in stereo, and the highlights of that recording were issued on a record. When Bill Hoole listened to the complete recordings he was thrilled to regain the excitement of the journey and it was interesting to find that, without any prompting, he was able to identify accurately many locations from different sounds that he heard. Shortly before he retired from BR and took up more leisurely employment, as a driver on the Festiniog Railway, Bill Hoole wrote for the record sleeve:

> Driving steam locomotives has been my life and has always had a thrill for me. On the footplate the metallic ring from the rods and the rail joints blend with the sounds of the exhaust beats, quick- ening as speed builds up, and the sounds of the coal shovel and water feeds. All this develops into a wonderful symphony of music to my ears. Great satisfaction is derived from making up time lost from some unseemly delay. This often meant long stretches with speeds of 80 or 90 or more which, with heavy trains behind, added to the pleasure of achievement from good teamwork by fireman and driver and gave a feeling of zest and power, a reward that only high speed with safety can bring.

In the years before 1959 I had made evocative and historically valuable recordings of locomotives in everyday service with passenger and freight trains on main and branch lines, heard from on board trains, on the footplate, or at various lineside locations throughout Britain. A unique LMS locomotive, the 0–10–0 *Lickey Banker*, was recorded at work in 1955, shortly before its withdrawal. Unfortunately it was never possible to record the LNER Garratt locomotive, but several subsequent visits to Bromsgrove and the Lickey Incline were unfailingly rewarding. On LMS lines further north the climb to Shap was one of my favourite locations, frequently visited by day and night, though I lost many opportunities because of the vagaries of Westmorland weather. In 1958 I spent the August Bank Holiday weekend beside the line between Tebay and Shap Wells. As it turned out, Derek and David Cross were also there, taking innumerable photographs, although we didn't actually meet until years later.

ABOVE *Class 9F No. 92155 roars over the top of the Lickey incline after two miles of climbing on a gradient of 1 in 37.*

The Shap moorlands were wonderfully peaceful before the motorway arrived although, particularly when the wind blew from the west, the ceaseless whine of traffic on the existing A6 road could be heard in the background, by day or night, and it was impossible to attempt any recordings on the climb between Penrith and Shap station, where the railway runs closer to the road. Sound recordists are obviously particularly affected by and sensitive to unwanted noise, but noise pollution – especially from aircraft and road traffic – is a seriously intrusive curse of modern life. By comparison the noise of railways is insignificant, particularly on electrified lines laid with continuously welded rails, since the sounds of passing trains are intermittent and of short duration.

In the spring of 1959 I made a return visit to the West Highland line, with recently acquired stereo recording equipment which, though heavy, cumbersome and somewhat temperamental, added new qualities to the recordings. John Adams and Patrick Whitehouse, of BBC *Railway Roundabout* fame, had arranged for the sleeping-car trains in both directions between Glasgow and Fort William to be double-headed by NBR 4–4–0 locomotives, *Glen Loy* and *Glen Falloch*. I successfully recorded the rousing and unforgettable sounds of those two locomotives at work at Ardlui, Tyndrum, Bridge of Orchy and, most spectacular of all, at a location in a wide valley between Bridge of Orchy

ABOVE *The peace of the moorlands is shattered as 9F No. 92033 struggles past Shap Wells with bulk ammonia. Class 4 No. 75037 pushes at the rear.*

and Tyndrum, where, hugging the lower contours of mountains rising to heights between 2897 and 3452 ft, the line climbs round a horse-shoe curve with a final gradient of 1 in 55, that continues for $2\frac{1}{2}$ miles to Tyndrum summit. Trains on the Dunblane–Oban line which served Tyndrum (lower) station could be clearly heard at Tyndrum (upper) station, on the West Highland line; consequently it was possible to make some most effective stereo recordings when train times on the two lines coincided.

During the next few days I made successful visits to other Scottish railway locations. At Ballinluig a Caledonian 0–4–4 tank engine, with rhythmically thumping brake pump, detached a coach from a main-line train in the station and set off down the branch line to Aberfeldy. Isolated Killin junction was inaccessible except by rail, but the activities of a Caledonian tank engine at Killin station, fussing around with the branch-line train and leaving for the junction, made a charming sound picture of a rural branch line, completed when a Caledonian 0–6–0 was heard, taking a mixed goods and passenger train towards the junction. LNER locomotives made interesting sounds, to a background of seagulls, on the steep climb out from Montrose and, just beyond the summit of that climb, I heard the 'Aberdonian' and other trains one evening, near Usan signal box. I spent some hours less successfully at Wormit, where my attempts to record trains crossing the Tay bridge from Dundee were often thwarted by a combination of unfavourable weather and various unwanted background noises.

Patrick Whitehouse and John Adams provided another opportunity to hear some vintage engines when, in 1960, two Caledonian 4–4–0s were specially rostered to head the morning mail train between Blair Atholl and Inverness, and arrangements were made for the Great North of Scotland Railway 4–4–0 *Gordon Highlander* to work some passenger trains between Aviemore and Craigellachie. At the end of 1960 I made a long-promised visit to the Carlisle–Edinburgh line, the Waverley route. The weather was arctic, roads were treacherous and the low temperatures affected recording equipment, so outdoor recording was impossible. I made two return journeys by train over the whole line, during one of which I travelled on the footplate of a class A1 Pacific, from Hawick to Carlisle. The weather was at its worst, with a bitter wind driving intermittent snow across the tracks and, although the engine's cab was comparatively spacious, conditions on the footplate were somewhat uncomfortable, especially for the driver who, whenever he leant out of the cab, had his head and shoulders frozen, while his legs were roasted every time the firehole door opened, as it frequently had to be on the long, steep climb

from Hawick to Whitrope tunnel. That journey vividly illustrated the hard work and devotion to duty required of engine crews who had to work trains over the Waverley route.

As anticipated, the section of line on the northbound climb between Newcastleton and Whitrope summit had some of the best recording locations I had found anywhere in Britain. Sheep and lambs joined moorland birds to provide a gentle background to the stirring sounds of passing engines, slogging uphill past the lonely little station at Steele Road which was situated midway on the continuous 1 in 75 10-mile climb from Newcastleton to Riccarton. It was a somewhat eerie place at night, when the station and the signal box, which was only manned by the porter-signalman when required, were in darkness and innumerable owls hooted mournfully from nearby forest plantations. If the wind was favourable the freight trains could be heard for many minutes, climbing away across the moors to Riccarton, an even lonelier place, far from any road and only accessible by rail. It was deprived of its status as a junction when, in October 1956, passenger services were withdrawn on the branch line from Hexham, and two years later, when freight services were also

ABOVE *Preserved Great North of Scotland Railway No. 49 'Gordon Highlander'*
at Auchengray in October 1965.
RIGHT *V2 class No. 60816 on the Waverley route near Riccarton Junction 1965.*

withdrawn, the line was finally closed. In earlier years Riccarton Junction was a close-knit railway community, provided with a Co-operative shop on the station platform, to which all supplies were brought by train. In early NBR days the inhabitants attended Sunday worship in the engine shed; subsequently, special church trains were run to Hawick and Newcastleton on alternate Sundays. The stationmaster established a post office in the waiting room and if someone was seriously ill, a locomotive was often sent to fetch a doctor, who travelled back to Riccarton on the footplate!

On the Waverley route the syncopated three-cylinder exhaust beat of the LNER V2 class locomotives was frequently heard at various locations. These maids of all work, equally adept at hauling passenger or freight trains, demonstrated an ability to produce an extraordinary variety of sounds and rhythms, according to the condition of the engine and the way in which it was worked.

Diesel locomotives soon began to replace the V2s and other steam locomotives on the Waverley route. The last V2 worked over the line in 1966 and in June of that year I made my final visit to the line. In 1963 the Beeching Report had described the Waverley route as the biggest loss-maker on BR. Then in 1966, BR's Chairman announced that retention of the line could no longer be justified and passenger services would cease in 1967, despite the fact

that, in 1966, an average of more than 8000 passengers a week had used the line during the winter and nearly 13 000 a week had used it during the summer.

The Scottish TUCC (Transport Users' Consultative Committee) strongly urged retention of the line and a government report on future development in the Borders recommended that, rather than considering the line's future on a purely commercial basis, its costs should be compared with its social benefits. Vigorous protests were made locally and at the House of Commons and a petition with more than 11 000 signatures was handed in to number 10 Downing Street, but the bureaucrats were unmoved and Transport Minister Richard Marsh announced that the line would definitely close in January 1969. The final train, the night sleeper to London, left Edinburgh on the night of 5 January 1969. At Newcastleton a reverend gentleman arranged a sit-in on the track that night and was charged with obstructing the train. The Edinburgh–Carlisle line, which had served the community for 120 years, was finally destroyed. Hawick gained doubtful distinction as the largest Scottish town more than 40 miles distant from a railhead, and another large area of Great Britain was deprived of the benefits of a railway service. Scotland suffered severely as a result of the Beeching Report, but fortunately some of the most drastic of the doctor's recommendations, for the country as a whole, have not yet been implemented, and indeed some have since been reversed.

In the spring of 1964 I had another opportunity to make recordings on the footplates of various locomotives working passenger and freight trains, first on the fearsomely graded and wonderfully scenic Central Wales line between Knighton and Llanelli, and later in Scotland. My first stop was Wales, where as usual the enginemen offered cheerful hospitality and co-operation, and told me of their problems in working over that difficult line, especially in the unpleasant conditions encountered at the time, when heavy rain dripped and drove on to the footplate, to the especial discomfort of the endlessly hard-working fireman, and slippery rails and strong cross winds called for all the skills of the driver to avoid stalling with a heavy train on steep, curving gradients. The single-track tunnels gave shelter from the wind and rain but filled the cab with choking fumes which, one driver told me, were almost insufferable for the crew of a banking engine at the rear of a train. Within a

TOP RIGHT *Stanier class 5 No. 45423 makes a volcanic departure from Ayr Station with a Glasgow train in October 1965.*

short while the Central Wales line was to be deliberately starved of traffic, by
diversion of cross-country freight trains, but closure recommendations were
not implemented and, mercifully, the line is still open to passengers.

From Wales I went to Scotland, where several A4 class Pacific locomotives
had been given an opportunity for a splendid swan-song, working Glasgow–
Aberdeen express trains. Journeys on A4 Pacifics with the 'St Mungo' and
'Bon Accord' expresses, to and from Aberdeen, were just as exciting as earlier
footplate trips on those and other engines, on the east coast main line.

Scotland was a haven for steam locomotives in the mid-1960s, and in
Ayrshire, for instance, many were well maintained and in regular service.
During 1965 and later, I spent many fascinating hours, by day and night,
beside the Ayr–Stranraer line and other BR lines. Steam working around Ayr
was not confined to BR, for steam locomotives were still vigorously working
on the railways of several then busy collieries. At Barony colliery, near Auchin-
leck, an 0–4–0 saddle tank engine, built by Neilson of Glasgow in 1885, was hard
at work. On the extensive lines around Waterside colliery, more modern engines,

sometimes with two engines to a train, were vociferously hauling heavy trains. Preserved vintage Scottish engines were put into service on special occasions, such as the Highland Railway centenary in August 1965, when I recorded Highland Railway locomotive No. 103, the Jones Goods 4–6–0, at work with a train of Caledonian coaches, between Forres and Inverness.

Almost my last footplate recording on BR was made on board 'Britannia' Pacific No. 70016 *Ariel*, which, assisted by a class 5 4–6–0 as pilot engine, left Ayr at 4.26 on a June morning in 1966 with the 367-ton London–Stranraer boat train. It was my first footplate trip on a double-headed train and it was exceptionally interesting to observe the expert way in which the crews of the two engines worked in harmony, with the engines' whistles as their only direct means of communication. As always, that footplate journey made an unforgettable impression which I hoped might, at least in some way, be shared by others if they listened to the recording.

My final footplate journey in this country was on a class 9F 2–10–0 with a freight train between Carlisle and Hellifield, on the persistently threatened

ABOVE *Preserved Highland Railway No. 103, the 'Jones Goods', pulls away from Upper Port Glasgow in April 1965.*

TOP RIGHT *9F No. 92056 climbs to Aisgill Summit on the Settle–Carlisle line.*

RIGHT *Two J27s sit under the smoke vents of Sunderland shed.*

Settle–Carlisle line. It was interesting to find that the crew shared my disgust at the shabby way in which the remaining British steam locomotives were being treated. The declining years of steam power in Britain were certainly extremely depressing. Filthy engines, in deplorable mechanical condition, were to be seen limping around without name-plates, sometimes lacking external fittings and often with chalked numbers in place of plates that had been stolen by so-called enthusiasts, or removed to prevent such thefts. This was surely no way to treat machines which had so faithfully served the railways, and had been so much admired by railwaymen and others. In Britain, many quite modern engines were scrapped in frantic haste, long before the end of their useful lives.

Railways elsewhere in Europe adopted a more economical and less hysterical policy, maintaining many of their steam locomotives in excellent mechanical and external condition and making good use of them on various services, well into the 1970s.

I have always lived within sight or sound of a railway, and the sounds of steam trains, particularly when heard during the night, were somehow reassuringly comforting. They were an integral and important part of the world that I grew up in, and were sadly missed when they disappeared.

My journey to Scotland from East Anglia was, nevertheless, comfortable, punctual and much quicker in 1987 than in earlier times, and it was still possible to avoid London by changing trains at Peterborough, much improved by the long-promised reconstruction which removed a notorious speed restriction. Grantham, scene of so many recording sessions, had long since lost its engine sheds. On past Doncaster, York, Darlington and Durham – all prompting memories of past experiences and sadness at so many dilapidated buildings, rusting or vanished sidings and factory rail connections. During the whole journey north there was scant evidence of any freight traffic, and, thinking back to nights spent beside this line, when express freight, parcels, mail and sleeping-car trains passed in quick succession, the idea that the east coast main line could be closed at night seemed unbelievable. It does sometimes seem that BR is in danger of becoming a single traffic railway, apparently making little effort to encourage freight traffic while placing undue emphasis on the needs of businessmen on expense accounts in first-class accommodation.

Edinburgh station was a revelation, with helpful information services, shopping arcades and bright buffets where refreshments were cheerfully and efficiently served. Travelling to Inverness (where the station has been similarly rejuvenated), and finally to the clean and welcoming little terminus at Wick, it was evident that ScotRail are making determined and successful efforts to improve the image of British railways. Stations were clean and well kept, unlike so many in other areas, trains were well cared for and staff were smart and helpful, providing adequate explanations for any unexpected delays. Cheerful girls operated a mini buffet on the Inverness–Wick line, particularly welcome on the early morning train that took me over the unfamiliar line, through some hauntingly beautiful country, to the far north of Scotland and the end of my journey.

The admirable efforts of railway workers and management are not, alone, enough to ensure a future for Britain's railways. The railways must also be given adequate finance to provide the safe, quick and reliable means of transport for which they are so well suited. In cases when trains are hopelessly overcrowded, delayed or cancelled, B R are unable to provide any form of relief service, because they are forced to operate with a bare minimum of facilities that allows no margin for back-up in any such circumstances.

The Channel Tunnel is one area which does offer exciting future possibilities for Britain's railways, but, however willing B R may be to exploit them, they cannot do so without money for capital investment. The French railways intend to link their side of the tunnel with a new high-speed line. When the trains reach Britain it seems that they will have to reduce speed and travel, over old existing tracks, to a terminus at Waterloo, where delays are already experienced on the congested approaches to the station.

The opportunities presented by the Channel Tunnel are just as important to Scotland as they are to the rest of Britain and it seems short-sighted to build the principal road–rail interchange terminal in the overcrowded south-east of England. If other interchange terminals were provided inland in England and in Scotland, freight traffic could travel direct by rail to and from the continent. North–south road traffic would be reduced and any new rail links to the terminals would take up less land than new motorways. It is now obviously deplorable that the Great Central main line, the only railway in Britain which was superbly engineered to take continental loading-gauge trains, was so thoughtlessly and ruthlessly run down and destroyed. Had it survived, it would have provided a valuable direct link between the tunnel and the Midlands and the north of England and Scotland.

ABOVE *The line which proved that railway preservation was not just a pipe dream. No. 1 'Talyllyn' at Dolgoch Station on the pioneer Talyllyn Railway in North Wales.*

OPPOSITE *Near the end of its working life, Stanier 'Duchess' Pacific No. 46230 heads north with a mixed bag of parcel vans.*

British Railways Standard class 2 No. 78016 ventures off the beaten track in Scotland with the Garlieston branch goods train.

A Stephenson Locomotive Society special, with preserved locomotives 103 and 'Gordon Highlander', working hard at Glenwhilly in 1963. Both are now in the Glasgow Transport Museum.

FROM TOP

Stanier class 5 No. 45588 crosses Big Fleet viaduct on the Stranraer–Carlisle line.

One of many Scottish enthusiast specials that ran in the early 1960s: veteran Caledonian class 2F No. 57375 at Millisle in 1963.

Z class No. 30957 pushes a heavy eastbound train up to the Southern station at Exeter Central, its green coaches contrasting with the maroon of Western Region.

TOP *'Britannia' class No. 70036 at Garsdale, formerly known as Hawes Junction, on the Settle–Carlisle line.*

ABOVE *Stanier class 5 No. 45450 at Dillicar water troughs, heading northwards to Tebay and Shap.*

ABOVE
A 'Britannia' class Pacific on a northbound parcels train near Greenholm.

CENTRE
A southbound freight in the Lune Gorge, 1965.

BELOW
At Highscale, between Rise Hill Tunnel and Garsdale, on the Settle–Carlisle line.

ABOVE

Carnforth locomotive depot in the last years of steam. Dominating the scene is the coaling tower, once a familiar landmark at every major steam shed.

LEFT

Early days on the Bluebell Railway. With almost as many engines as coaches, this was hardly an authentic exercise in preservation! But it was great fun for all concerned.

LEFT
The Pulborough to Midhurst 'goods train' in June 1962, with a driver, fireman and guard employed, but no goods to carry.

BELOW LEFT
Before the era of preservation, a pannier tank is reduced to scrap at Swindon in March 1958.

BELOW
'Merchant Navy' class No. 35023 on the up 'Atlantic Coast Express' at Exeter Central in July 1957.

ABOVE 'Hall' class No. 5911 'Guild Hall' receives attention in the 'A' shop of the former GWR works at Swindon. In 1988 most of the workshops were demolished, but there are plans to re-establish steam overhaul facilities in one of the surviving buildings.

THE
SURVIVORS

— ∘ 6 ∘ —

ANDREW JOHNSTON

Mrs Thatcher, we are told, dislikes railways and never travels by train. John Betjeman, we know, loved them and went by train as often as possible. These two extreme views reflect an emotional history, in which the railway itself has become symbolic of a whole way of life, with its tradition of public service and of things built to last. Even in today's unromantic age of diesel and electric high-speed trains, there is still for some a hint of adventure about the start of a long train journey.

I was exposed to the romance of railways at an early age. As a child of the 1950s I was taken on holiday, not by a mere motor-car but by big, noisy steam locomotives, an experience never to be forgotten. Our journey from Brighton in Sussex to Mawgan Porth in north Cornwall took all day. It was filled with interest, a growing sense of excitement and the certainty that we were on an epic voyage of discovery.

The images remain sharp and clear thirty years on: glimpses of the English Channel as we ran along the south coast, the *Queen Elizabeth* or *Queen Mary* towering above the railway in their Southampton dry dock, the spire of Salisbury Cathedral, and engines everywhere! Each one had a shape and character of its own, but by far the most impressive and memorable were the big express engines of the Pacific type. A steady procession of huge hissing green monsters passed the carriage window on 'Up' trains from the west, bearing names to stir the spirit: *Fighter Pilot*, *Spitfire*, *Hurricane*; majestic

TOP *A T9 class pauses at Camelford (for Boscastle and Tintagel) on the wild and winding North Cornwall line to Padstow and the sea.*

ABOVE *'Battle of Britain' class Pacific No. 34056 'Croydon' pounds up a stretch of 1 in 80 near Milborne Port on the Waterloo–Exeter main line in August 1964.*

names of shipping lines: *Cunard White Star, Orient Line, Lamport and Holt Line*; and the names of West Country towns just to prove you were going on holiday: *Wadebridge, Ottery St Mary, Torrington.*

On the edge of Dartmoor a windswept change of trains at Okehampton took us on to the long winding branch line to Padstow and the Atlantic coast. Here the memories are of night falling as we shuddered to a halt in exposed and empty stations – Camelford, Delabole, St Kew Highway – strange, exciting Cornish names on enamel signs flickering in the light of swaying oil lamps, and Cornish voices calling out in the darkness. Then a distant whistle and the sound of our engine fighting for grip on the slippery rails as we set off into the blast of a westerly gale straight off the sea. Live coals, hurled from the chimney as the engine fought against the gradient, rattled on the carriage roof or lay glowing beside the track, while inside our cosy compartment the comforting glow of the reading lamps was reflected in varnished woodwork and framed pictures of the seaside. Then at last other lights were reflected in the waters of the Camel estuary. The engine no longer laboured but drifted along, clattering over the iron bridge spanning Little Petherick Creek and into Padstow station with the smell of steam, drifting smoke, hot oil and salt air, for out there unseen in the darkness was the Atlantic Ocean. Tomorrow the holidays would begin, but for me the very best part was already over.

Other shorter visits to my aunt in West Sussex involved trips on the branch line to Midhurst, with ancient tank engines and equally ancient coaches painted red or green in which you often found yourself pushed rather than pulled by the engine.

It never struck me as odd to be transported by a machine that ran on coal and water in an age of electrical gadgets. True, our local electric trains on the Brighton line had no engine hissing steam at the front end, but still in amongst them were black clanking goods engines with tall chimneys and big domes perched on their boilers.

It couldn't last. One year we went to Cornwall by another route on what had been the Great Western Railway from Paddington. The engine went uninspected in the rush to get a seat, but as we headed westward it seemed to me that something wasn't quite right. There were no clouds of drifting steam to block the view. I opened the window with its leather strap and, ignoring the warning sign above, I leaned out. In place of the normal and instant smut in the eye, I was met by gusts of hot air smelling of oil. The sound was all wrong as well – no chuffing, just a sort of low growl. I had met, but not yet seen, my first diesel engine.

After this things began to move fast. In 1963 a beaming, well-fed-looking gentleman had his picture in all the papers. He was a doctor called Beeching from ICI and he was planning some changes for the railway. To cure the ailing finances of the railway system he hit upon the idea of closing down about half of it. All my favourite lines were to be torn up and sold for scrap; steam would have to go, of course, and not just the old engines, with tall chimneys. They went first, but then it was the turn of all those big, green Pacifics. Many lost their name-plates and became merely numbers. Then, after lingering on in filthy condition for a few months, they were gone. The plan was stark and simple: the railway as we knew it was going to be destroyed wholesale and, with government backing, the private road-haulage industry was to take most of its traffic. We would be left with a basic network of trunk lines for commuters, business travellers and what remained of the goods traffic. It was a bad time to be a railway worker: the Beeching plan involved the loss of more than 100,000 jobs as well.

ABOVE *Midhurst in 1951 with M7 class No. 30049 and two vintage coaches. Today every trace of this station has vanished.*

RIGHT *Dr Richard Beeching prepares to cut the railway down to size.*

The full impact of it all came home to me when in 1964, as part of a photographic project at art college, I visited Guildford engine shed. Its smoke-blackened interior was full of neglected-looking steam locomotives grouped round the central turntable. Some were in steam, most were cold. On one track sat a bulky Q1 class, a rather ugly but practical design built for wartime traffic. Its centre driving wheels had been removed and a fitter was attending to a damaged bearing. 'I don't know why I'm bothering to do this,' he told me. 'It's going for scrap in a week's time and I'm being made redundant next month.' It was a depressing visit which left me wondering what, if anything, would be left of the system when Beeching had finished with it.

There was some resistance, but most opposition was half-hearted and unco-ordinated. A mood of fatalism prevailed and the Minister of Transport, Ernest Marples (formerly of road builders Marples-Ridgeway), was happy to give his blessing to closure after closure. Many expected a change of policy when a Labour government was returned in 1964, but it was not to be. Transport Minister Barbara Castle was no friend of the railways either, and the rapid decline continued. There was deep and lasting bitterness among the railwaymen, who felt that 'their' government had betrayed them. Years later in an interview, Lord Beeching, as he had become, expressed his regret that more lines had not been closed, despite the fact that his surgery did not have the desired effect on the railway's finances and huge losses continued.

Against this trend, a few people were trying to save a little of what was being lost. In 1951 the Talyllyn, a Welsh narrow-gauge line, had been saved by a preservation society. Its story inspired the classic Ealing comedy film *The Titfield Thunderbolt* made in 1952. It was one of the first films I was ever taken to and made a deep and lasting impression.

It is the story of a group of villagers who refuse to accept the closure of their branch line and fight to reopen it. The villagers, led by the vicar, are

ABOVE *In this classic picture of steam's last unloved years, a Q1 class has its smokebox emptied at Guildford shed in 1964.*

TOP RIGHT *The film that inspired so many preservationists, 'The Titfield Thunderbolt', was itself inspired by the rescue of the Talyllyn.*

RIGHT *The first standard-gauge line to be saved from scrap was the Bluebell Railway in Sussex. 'P' class No. 323 is seen on the day the line reopened, 3 July 1960.*

enthusiastic if entirely ignorant about the running of a railway, but manage to raise the money from the local millionaire, played by Stanley Holloway, to buy the line. Bureaucrats from the Ministry, and the local 'wide boys' with their rival bus service, do their best to stop the plan, but it all ends happily, if improbably. The railway and the enthusiasts are victorious.

The film was an inspiration to many; perhaps it really could be done on a full-size line. In Sussex a group set out to buy part of the East Grinstead to Lewes line. In 1960 a 5-mile section became the Bluebell Railway, and, with

two small engines and two coaches, the group set out to prove that they too could run a railway.

For most branch lines, however, there was no reprieve. In the real world the Stanley Holloway character with the blank cheque proved elusive, and railways are expensive things to buy.

The Midhurst branch lingered on into 1964 with a steam goods train three times a week (passenger trains had finished in the 1950s). Then one day a diesel engine replaced the usual steam engine. 'This is the end,' I thought, and in a few months it was. The demolition gang slowly worked their way down the line past my aunt's house. With oxyacetylene cutting gear they hacked the rails into handy lengths for melting down. Soon nature was busy taking back the well-kept trackbed. Padstow went shortly afterwards, and in 1967 the last few Southern steam locomotives were towed away, with messages of farewell chalked on their sides, to some far-off cemetery.

ABOVE *Just two of the many classes of steam locomotive that were entirely wiped out. 'Z' class tank No. 30953 with Drummond '700' class No. 30317 at Exmouth Junction Shed.*

RIGHT *One of the fortunate few: Midland Railway single No. 118, preserved in its original livery.*

Steam retreated into its last stronghold west of the Pennines, but I felt no desire to go and see its death throes. The railway magazines were full of cries for help ('Your last chance to save a Stanier Class 8'). I sent my donation, but without much conviction that it would help. 11 August 1968 came and went; the very last steam train had run; the last few locomotives were struck off the list, and it was all over. 'Today British Rail ran out of steam', 'It's goodbye to the puff puffs', 'End of the line for the puffers' – the press said a jaunty farewell and turned to more important topics: 'New motorway opens early', 'More cash for roads, says Minister'. Steam was dead.

Slowly the realisation came that whatever had survived in museums and on a few preserved railways like the Bluebell Line was the final tally. There would be no more 'last chances'. I bought a book on preserved locomotives and read with growing dismay a list of the survivors – there were so few of them! Classes that had numbered hundreds of locomotives were reduced to one or two, and there were huge gaps where entire classes had slipped away into oblivion. Of roughly 17 000 engines that had been removed from British Railways, less than 200 survived. How could so many have been broken up – and where had they all gone to die?

I saw and kept a half-page picture in a Sunday paper which helped to answer the second question. A rusting steam engine with broken windows was

shown with a caption explaining that it was one of more than 200 in a scrapyard at Barry, in south Wales. Once it had worked on the Southern Railway near my home. When photographed it was under sentence of death, awaiting the executioner. Today, in as-new condition, it works on the preserved Severn Valley line near Birmingham. What happened in between is almost like a fairy story, which begins with two brothers, Billy and Dai Woodham, who had a scrap-metal business in south Wales.

It had been traditional practice for the railways to break up old locomotives themselves, but the flood of withdrawn engines in the 1960s was beyond their capacity and outside scrap merchants were invited to tender for the work. The Woodhams decided to have a go. Slowly their yard began to fill up with British Railway history: 'Kings' and 'Castles' from the Great Western Railway, 'Jubilees' and 'Black 5s' from the London, Midland & Scottish, and from the Southern came the magnificent monsters from my childhood, the 'Merchant Navy', 'West Country' and 'Battle of Britain' class Pacifics. There were others: humble tank engines, heavy goods engines, large and small, old and new, one built as long ago as 1905, one as recently as 1960. By the end of steam in 1968 the yard was full. Many had been broken up during the same period, but work then switched to the thousands of redundant wagons that were coming out of service as British Railways abandoned its goods traffic to the heavy lorry.

So there they sat, 221 steam engines tightly packed together in long rows within sight of the holiday beaches of Barry Island near Cardiff. Silently they waited for the final encounter with the gas cutter. Almost all were complete, some had steamed to their last resting place, and there they continued to sit as first the weeds and then the rust took hold.

After those last hectic years of steam, the enthusiasts drew a deep breath and looked at what was left. About half a dozen branch lines were preserved and, after an unsteady start, seemed to be popular with the public, who would pay for 5 miles of steam-train travel for old times' sake. The promoters of one early scheme, the Dart Valley Railway, invited the executioner himself to perform the christening. Dr Beeching proclaimed the line open, with the observation that if he had not first closed it he could not then be reopening it! However, perhaps despite Dr Beeching's good wishes, the railway survived to become firmly established as one of the pioneers of the preservation movement.

RIGHT *Lines of rusting locomotives at Barry Docks in 1972, four years after the end of steam on British Railways.*

The lines had the very minimum number of engines needed to maintain a service. Most were small tank engines well suited to the job of pulling a couple of coaches along at a pace slow enough to spin out the ride. British Rail and the county councils looked on these lines with a detached, slightly amused but very jaundiced eye. They were, after all, run by amateurs, commonly dismissed as 'overgrown schoolboys playing trains'. But the British public seemed prepared to give the little lines the benefit of the doubt.

The explosion of the tourist railway business has been astonishing, surpassing the wildest dreams of the early pioneers. The rise of the preserved railways has mirrored the decline of Britain's heavy industries, notably coal, steel and shipbuilding. Left high and dry by the ebbing tide of manufacturing industry were skilled men and women who suddenly found themselves with nothing to do. Young people who in the 1960s would have found jobs now, in an era of mass unemployment, had none to go to – the booming service industries could only employ a fraction. To the railway workers who had lived through the Beeching era this was nothing new; they'd seen it all before. But

for the preserved railways it meant an influx of skilled volunteers glad to do anything other than simply draw the dole and sit at home. In addition there were armies of young people on job creation schemes who could clear undergrowth or dig ditches. But above all there were customers, tens of thousands of people, all of them wanting to experience something that would remind them of the good old days when 'British was best' and it seemed that things were built to last.

Throughout the 1970s and 1980s the preservation movement has expanded. Prophets of doom regularly predicted disaster and collapse. A common belief was that any new line was a rival that would only dilute the available number of passengers. In practice the market has grown roughly in line with the number of new steam railways, although there must be a limit to how far expansion can go.

Given a hardworking unpaid labour force and sufficient funds, there are three additional basic ingredients which have to be obtained before you can open a railway: track to run on, coaches to ride in, and engines to pull the coaches and attract the crowds. These have to be steam engines for the 'mix' to work properly. Track and coaches are easy – British Rail will sell them to you. But where do you buy steam engines when British Rail have none left?

The answer lay with Woodham Brothers back at Barry. Word of their host of stored engines began to spread and, undeterred by rust and missing parts, groups of enthusiasts began to buy, remove and restore them. Slowly at first, then with growing frequency, engines emerged from their long hibernation and came back to do again the job they had been built for. They gave the preservationists a second chance.

My first encounter with the silent army of locomotives at Barry's No. 1 Dock was in the early 1970s. Standing on three groups of sidings and spread out over many acres, the sight of more than 200 decaying engines was one never to be forgotten, an elephants' graveyard of gigantic proportions. To walk between row after row of them was an eerie experience. The signs of their working life were still clear in spite of the ravages of the salty air: tenders still with the last few shovelfuls of their final load of coal, smokeboxes still full of ash that should have been emptied by one of the now-redundant army of shed staff, and in the boxes sand that once stopped the driving wheels slipping. Above the wheels towered cabs, tanks and boilers red with rust but still bearing the crest of British Railways, a lion and a wheel – symbolic of pride and power.

TOP RIGHT *Class 9F No. 92212 at Barry in 1975, marked by its prospective rescuer.*

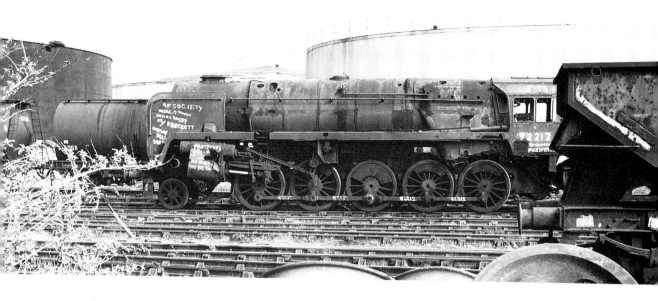

On some the peeling paint even revealed the names of the original owners: 'GWR' and 'Southern'. (Today's double arrow BR symbol never found its way on to a main-line steam engine.) Below the waistline all were plastered in a thick protective coating of oil, coal dust, ash and other by-products of the steam age – a legacy of their final, unloved years when maintenance was almost non-existent. On the driving wheels of my beloved Southern Pacifics, strangely designed with holes not spokes, the muck lay in a pattern of radiating lines thrown out from the centre while running at speed, like geological evidence of prehistoric activity. Now they were rooted to the spot with brambles twisting in and out of the holes. It was strange to come face to face with those wheels again; from ground level they seemed even bigger than I remembered them from childhood.

How sad, I thought, walking among these legendary giants, that soon men would come with cutting gear and reduce them to piles of anonymous scrap metal. These same men were already busy on rows of mineral wagons only a few yards away. The roaring gas jets threw sheets of sparks and the crash of falling metal punctuated the silence. Some engines carried crudely painted but heartfelt slogans: 'Steam for ever', 'Save me', 'King of Edgehill', 'Please don't let me die'. But here and there were other more strident messages: 'Avon Valley Railway – keep off', 'Reserved DVR. Do not take parts', 'Sold SVR'.

So it was that a minor miracle took place, and from these early beginnings an entire fleet of locomotives came back from the brink of oblivion to a new life. Who could have guessed then that almost all of them would survive? The supply of wagons for scrap was never-ending. With every closed coal mine, goods depot or country siding that fell to the recession or switched to road haulage, there were more unwanted wagons. They were quick and easy to cut up, and Woodhams preferred to let the more complicated job of breaking up the steam engines wait for the proverbial rainy day when other work was scarce. This decision has made an ordinary scrap merchant (which Dai Woodham always insists he is) into a celebrity.

It is said that buying a steam locomotive is the easy part and from then on it gets harder. In terms of finance a modest overhaul today can cost ten times the price of an entire locomotive as bought from British Railways in the 1960s. The restoration of a big engine from Barry these days will leave very little change from £100 000, and many projects have ground to a halt for lack of money.

In the wake of the preservationists there has grown up a sort of cottage industry in locomotive parts. Those that survive are swapped and traded, those that don't are manufactured. A shrinking railway system produced plenty of work for scrap merchants but not much for builders. One by one the great workshops of the old railway companies have closed, but at the same time a new kind of locomotive works has grown up. The bigger preserved railways and a few enterprising private engineering firms have equipped themselves with the discarded tools of the steam age and as a result are able to mend or replace locomotive parts. The skills needed are being kept alive, and there seems no reason why steam should not have an unlimited life.

Perhaps the best example of what can be achieved is the *Duke of Gloucester*, prototype for what would have been a new 1950s express class. The policy of abandoning steam meant that no more were built, and after initial proposals for preservation this unique and important locomotive was sent for scrap. One cylinder was cut off for exhibition in the Science Museum and, after losing another to even up the weight, it took what should have been its last journey. It was bought by Woodhams, sent to the wrong scrapyard by mistake and almost cut up, but found its way eventually to Barry in 1967. For years it was ignored by preservationists who saw it as beyond hope of recovery. Then a group was formed with the aim of returning the *Duke* to its original condition and it left Barry in 1974. Twelve years later, shining in its Brunswick Green livery and back in steam, this historic engine was renamed by His Royal Highness the present Duke of Gloucester. The years between had involved the skills of draughtsmen, pattern makers, iron founders and forgers, machinists,

TOP RIGHT *Tribute to the Barry preservationists: the rebuilt 'Duke of Gloucester', seen here in 1986 on the Great Central Railway.*

fitters and painters. Some were paid, some donated their time; help came from companies and individuals, enthusiast volunteers and the general public, whose imagination had been captured by this example of determination.

It is easy to forget how hard the task of returning a derelict locomotive to steam can be. It usually has to be dismantled to its component parts; these are then cleaned, grit-blasted to remove the years of rust, and painted. This is the easy and relatively inexpensive part. Worn-out bearings have to be replaced, missing parts found or made – and the costs begin to rise. Years of going home with dirty hands, bruised knuckles, wet clothes and a sense of frustration with tools that don't fit and nuts that won't unscrew, take their toll on the volunteers. Against this must be set the feeling of shared determination creating firm and lasting friendships, the learning of new skills and the satisfaction of doing a complex and demanding job properly.

One of the best features of railway preservation is its ability to cut through social and class differences. On a job like locomotive restoration you can find bricklayers and bank managers working side by side. In their dirty boiler suits it's hard to distinguish the marketing manager from the plumber, or the travel agent from the locomotive fitter. In this situation, if there is a gaffer it's going to be the fitter. At length the day arrives when that pile of rusting steel comes to life, takes its first gasp of steam and moves under its own power. The years of toil are all forgotten in the excitement of that first steaming.

The return of the Barry engines transformed the preserved railway business. First it was small branch-line tank engines that attracted most buyers, then bigger tender locos, and soon even the largest classes in the yard were being snapped up. After protracted and expensive overhauls, mostly done without proper workshop facilities, the returning heroes began to breathe fire and live again. Some more established preservationists took a dim view of 'Barry wrecks' as they were dubbed. But when transformed into revenue-earning locomotives they became harder to dismiss as a waste of time and money.

The first generation of preservationists set out to save what they could of the steam railways they grew up with, and they are now handing over to a younger generation, some of whom were not even born when steam ended. For many of this age group the early diesel and electric locomotives are as important as steam was to mine. The new machines I regarded as characterless, evil-smelling usurpers of steam's rightful place are, in their turn, now being saved and cared for. Future generations will probably preserve and cherish examples of their replacement, the universal InterCity 125.

ABOVE *The Southern Railway's S15 class owes its survival to Barry. Here No. 30845 passes under the gantry signal at Yeovil Junction in 1962.*

RIGHT *Only the tall Midland Hotel (between the signals in the background) survives of this Somerset and Dorset scene at Bournemouth West.*

152

At the same time, however, new generations are getting hooked on the image of a steam age they never experienced. Thanks to the work of photographers such as Ivo Peters, we are able to relive in every detail the last years of steam's golden age. Long closed lines like the Somerset & Dorset are better known in death than they ever were in life. The number of books written, films made, talks given and exhibitions mounted continues to rise as the legend parts company with the memory and acquires a life of its own.

For a time after the end of steam there was a total ban on any ideas of running preserved locomotives on the main line. There was a belief that the modern image would suffer; and perhaps there was also a fear that a whiff of the old romance would remind the public of how dull rail travel had become.

The ban was only lifted when BR Chairman Richard Marsh grudgingly allowed an experimental steam-hauled run which proved phenomenally successful. When Marsh was succeeded as Chairman of BR in 1976 by Peter Parker, suddenly the railway had an enthusiastic champion, a man who believed in his industry and what he was selling. With Peter Parker British Rail found a human face, and during his enlightened reign railway preservation began to acquire respectability.

Before long BR were even running their own steam excursions on selected provincial routes. Having discarded all their own locomotives, they hired examples from York's newly opened railway museum and from private preservationists like the Severn Valley Railway. The opening of the National Railway Museum in York's old locomotive depot in 1975 gave preservation a tremendous boost. Railways were becoming firmly established as part of our heritage and worthy of serious study. Working replicas of some of the most significant early locomotives were built for the National Museum at York, and one of Dai Woodham's engines, Merchant Navy Pacific *Ellerman Lines*, was bought back by the taxpayers who once owned it. In sectioned form it now reveals to visitors the inner workings of a steam locomotive.

All this official interest began to influence local councils with an eye for tourism. A preserved railway became an asset and local authorities without one began to look uneasily at their neighbours'. In the wake of the recession, areas of industrial wasteland were turned almost overnight into visitor centres

ABOVE *Preservationists learned vital footplate skills from drivers like Donald Beale, seen here with 'West Country' Pacific 'Combe Martin' at Bath shed.*

RIGHT *Preserved No. 4472 'Flying Scotsman' on a visit to Swindon in 1964.*

and heritage trails as the last vestiges of traditional industry were incorporated into the sunrise industry of tourism. Railways, with their ability to offer a ride to the visitor, are popular candidates for the treatment.

It is a process that can easily get out of control, producing what many see as an unhealthy situation, for a country cannot survive as a nation of museums. The past has to be protected, its lessons learned and respected, but it cannot be allowed to take over. The museums and visitor centres that mark the graves of traditional industries today can be rather sad places. They provide an afternoon's entertainment for the family and, in a few cases, a handful of jobs for former employees who now act as guides. But there is no disguising the bitterness behind the brave face put on for the visitor.

Most heavy industry involves a mixture of noise, dirt, danger and hard physical work. When it dies all that is left is a shell, a structure with its heart taken out. The machines may survive but the way of life they produced has gone. Many museums work well but some lose the dignity of the original and become mere playthings, safe, clean, quiet and unreal. The patrons of The Old Foundry wine bar, Pithead restaurant and Spinning Jenny boutique know nothing of the former inhabitants and the life they led.

By contrast the preserved railways do manage to keep the old atmosphere alive. There may be stories of the good old days being told down at the Railway Inn, but it's on the steam railway itself that the spirit seems to survive, even flourish. Driving and maintaining steam locomotives is the same demanding

job it always was and former railwaymen who miss the life can relive it to the full if they so wish. Preserved locomotives are not toys but big and potentially dangerous machines; the professionalism of railwaymen is as important as the devotion of the enthusiasts.

For the family out for the day, or for parties of children on an educational outing from school, a ride on one of the top preserved lines may be as close as they will ever get to a train. Many people who grow up with the car see no need even to consider rail travel. They may barely glance at the steam engine, fail to notice the rebuilt signal box, ignore the restored compartment coach with its window strap and seaside pictures, and miss most of the scenery. Yet the chances are that they will go away having enjoyed their trip and many return next summer. Visiting enthusiasts, on the other hand, will closely examine every detail, count every rivet head, criticise the colour of everything from gates to goods wagons and, if satisfied that all is as it should be, will also go away content.

Film producers come in search of period locations. Companies hire special trains to wine and dine clients; passers-by drop in to use the toilets or buy an ice-cream. So the railway earns its living and regains its place as an established part of the local community once again.

Today the preservation of railways is big business. The Severn Valley Railway in the West Midlands, for example, has an annual turnover of more than £1 million, and slowly but surely Big Brother BR has learned that the private lines are worth co-operating with. After years of grim-faced hostility from some of British Rail's most powerful mandarins, a new openness has come and with it a new breed of BR manager. Chris Green, the man who runs the Network South East empire, is on record as wanting to collaborate with the tourist railways. 'We need each other,' he said, referring to the situation on the truncated Isle of Wight system, where a preserved line is seeking to extend and reconnect itself to the one surviving BR line. Ten years ago no BR manager would have admitted to such sentiments in public, but such is the importance of tourism in today's de-industrialised economy that a steam railway linked to BR is now given the sort of status once enjoyed by companies with private goods sidings.

Preservation was born in Wales with the narrow-gauge Talyllyn. Once the idea took root, other small Welsh lines were revived. They have become as important a part of the Welsh tourist industry as historic castles and sandy

RIGHT *The Festiniog Railway returns in triumph to Blaenau Ffestiniog in 1982.*

beaches. It is one of the contradictions of modern life that the car, having helped to kill off so much of the railway system, now keeps alive the preserved lines. Even in wildest, remotest north Wales the car makes it possible to reach and ride on the little trains, and the first priority for any railway restoration plan these days is a big car park.

The most successful narrow-gauge line is the Festiniog in north Wales. Once it ran from the sea at Porthmadog to the slate quarries at Blaenau Ffestiniog. After it closed in the 1940s, part of its route was flooded by a dam for the electricity board. The lower section was reopened in stages by a preservation society, and after a long and ultimately successful fight for compensation, the railway set out to build a by-pass route involving construction of a spiral to gain height and a long tunnel. Its aim was to return to Ffestiniog. A dedicated band of 'deviationists' braved the Welsh mountain weather and carved out the new route, and the little train returned in triumph to its home town. Blaenau Ffestiniog, built on the slate industry, was in sad decline and the return of the railway was a much needed boost to its tourist trade. With help from the

council a joint station was built linking the narrow-gauge line to British Rail's under-used branch to the town. Everybody benefited and everybody was happy: local government, nationalised railway and private preserved railway had combined in a successful venture. It was a pointer to the future. The preservationists would no longer have to struggle on alone.

Soon standard-gauge schemes began to spring up with the aim not of preserving existing lines, but of rebuilding routes that had been torn up. All over the country railways are now being rebuilt, and many miles of erased track are having to be redrawn on the maps. In several cases local councils are co-operating and even helping to finance the work with grants.

The leader in this field has been the 'Watercress Line' in Hampshire, with 7 miles of railway rebuilt on the old formation to link their isolated base at Alresford with the main line at Alton. They owned the land but had to buy thousands of tons of track and ballast; the cost in money and man hours has been enormous, while the quantities of materials involved and the planning required would have daunted the professionals in BR. But this line was rebuilt by volunteers learning the hard way how to tackle each job. It was a fitting tribute to them all that the official reopening was performed in 1985 by the Transport Minister, David Mitchell, himself a member of a preserved line.

There can be no better example of the coming of age of the full-size preserved railway than the Bluebell Railway in Sussex, where it all began in 1960. Like many tourist lines the 5-mile Bluebell is an isolated length of track running from nowhere in particular to somewhere else. In a bold step the railway decided in 1975 to launch a scheme to extend northwards for 6 miles and link up again with British Rail at East Grinstead. The trackbed had almost all been sold off to private landowners; one station, West Hoathly, had been demolished and its site was earmarked for housing development; the county council was unimpressed and the National Farmers' Union was hostile. Things looked unpromising, to put it mildly.

Railway preservationists, however, don't seem to know when they're beaten. The West Hoathly station site was bought as a first step in the extension plan, and in the face of objections from all sides a major enquiry was held. The Railway put up an exhaustively researched plan proving its ability to build and run the extension, and the benefit to tourism that would follow. This was met by the full force of the landowning and farming establishments,

TOP RIGHT *In October 1964 the Bluebell Railway's 'North London' tank was on hire to contractors tearing up the line to East Grinstead – now being rebuilt!*

together with the council. Not surprisingly, the inspector recommended refusal, but everyone was in for a surprise. The then Environment Secretary, Patrick Jenkin, used his statutory power to overturn the inspector's recommendation. In his view the railway represented a major tourist centre, which would be improved by a link with the main line, and he considered this outweighed the arguments of the landowners. Now the Bluebell is heading north to East Grinstead with British Rail's Network South East manager ready to welcome it. As an added confirmation of government support for the project, the ceremonial re-laying of the first length of new track was performed by the Secretary of State for Transport on 13 March 1988.

The political climate may change and nothing is certain in the railway business, but the present government tends to see the preserved lines as good 'privatised' examples for British Rail to follow. The financial benefits of unpaid volunteer labour are easily forgotten in this simplistic view, but what they can teach BR has more to do with attitudes. Most preserved railways radiate pride, confidence and a positive view of the product they offer to the public. They are selling a ride rather than a destination, which is ultimately what BR also has to do. For wherever a train goes a car can go as well, and only if the ride can be made attractive enough will drivers be tempted to take the train.

There seems to be a revival of interest in railways. The Channel Tunnel will generate a huge volume of extra traffic, while many major cities are looking hard at some form of Metro system of trams. But today places like Midhurst, Padstow and hundreds of other towns can only be spectators in any railway revival, thanks to British Rail's senseless policy of selling off trackbed piece-meal for whatever price it would fetch.

The Victorian railway system began as a bewildering jumble of small private companies, many locked in battle with each other in the fight for supremacy. Slowly and painfully they were grouped into bigger and bigger companies before being lumped together in one nationalised network. Now the clock is running backwards.

Few industries have been so drastically reduced and the process may not be over by any means – the railways are having to fight to retain even their traditional freight traffic, such as coal and steel, and the road-haulage lobby remains as strong as ever. Meanwhile the preservationists have left us with the largest and most comprehensive living museum of an industry ever created. We must hope that future generations will care enough to look after it.

ABOVE *Railway preservation comes of age: the Secretary of State for Transport, Paul Channon, inaugurates the northern extension of the Bluebell Railway in March 1988.*

*Preserved Stanier Pacific 'Duchess of Hamilton' keeps alive the spirit of
the steam age with a dramatic display of power on the Settle–Carlisle line
in 1983.*

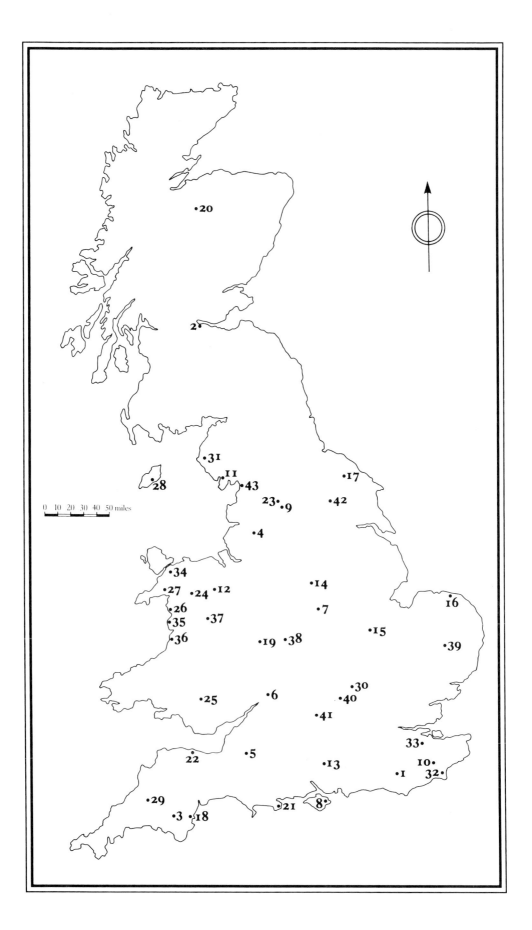

•20

2•

•31
11
•28   •43
         23••9   •17
                    •42
        •4

•34   •14
•27 •24 •12   •16
•26   •7
•35 •37   •15
•36   •19 •38   •39

•25   •6   •30
           •40
         •41
                  33•
•22 •5   •13   10•
         •1 32•
•29
•3 •18   •21 8•

0 10 20 30 40 50 miles

MAJOR PRESERVED RAILWAYS

———— o o o ————

STANDARD GAUGE

* Lines rebuilt from scratch after closure.

** Lines which are planning, building, or have already built extensions beyond their original length of preserved track.

1
BLUEBELL RAILWAY
Sheffield Park Station, Uckfield, East Sussex ☏ 082572 2370
5 miles **

2
BO'NESS & KINNEIL RAILWAY
Bo'ness Station, Union Street, Bo'ness, West Lothian ☏ 0506 822298
$3\frac{1}{2}$ *miles* *

3
BUCKFASTLEIGH & TOTNES STEAM RAILWAY
The Station, Buckfastleigh, Devon TQ11 0DZ ☏ 0364 42338
7 miles

4
EAST LANCASHIRE RAILWAY
Bury Bolton Street Station, Bolton Street, Bury, Lancashire BL9 0EY ☏ 061 7647790
4 miles

5
EAST SOMERSET RAILWAY
Cranmore Station, Shepton Mallet, Somerset ☏ 074 988417
2 miles **

6
GLOUCESTERSHIRE & WARWICKSHIRE RAILWAY
Toddington Station, Gloucestershire GL54 5DT ☏ 024269 346
3 miles

7

GREAT CENTRAL RAILWAY

Loughborough Central Station, Great Central Road, Loughborough, Leicestershire

☏ 0509 230726

$5\frac{1}{2}$ *miles* **

8

ISLE OF WIGHT STEAM RAILWAY

Haven Street Station, Ryde, Isle of Wight ☏ 0983 882204

$1\frac{1}{2}$ *miles* **

9

KEIGHLEY AND WORTH VALLEY RAILWAY

Haworth Station, Keighley, West Yorkshire BD22 8NJ ☏ 0535 45214

5 miles

10

KENT AND EAST SUSSEX RAILWAY

Tenterden Town Station, Tenterden, Kent ☏ 05806 2943

5 miles

11

LAKESIDE AND HAVERTHWAITE RAILWAY

Haverthwaite Station, Ulverston, Cumbria LA12 8AL ☏ 05395 31594

$3\frac{1}{2}$ *miles*

12

LLANGOLLEN RAILWAY

The Station, Abbey Road, Llangollen, Clwyd ☏ 0978 860951

2 miles *

13

MID-HANTS RAILWAY

Alresford Station, Alresford, Hampshire SO24 9JG ☏ 096273 4200

$10\frac{1}{2}$ *miles* **

14

MIDLAND RAILWAY CENTRE

Butterley Station, Ripley, Derbyshire ☏ 0773 570140

$3\frac{1}{2}$ *miles* **

15

NENE VALLEY RAILWAY

Wansford Station, Old North Road, Stibbington, Peterborough, Northants PE8 6LR

☏ 0780 782854

$7\frac{1}{2}$ *miles* **

16

NORTH NORFOLK RAILWAY

Sheringham Station, Sheringham, Norfolk ☎ 0263 822045

$5\frac{1}{4}$ *miles* **

17

NORTH YORKSHIRE MOORS RAILWAY

Pickering Station, Pickering, North Yorkshire YO18 7AJ ☎ 0751 72508

18 miles

18

PAIGNTON AND DARTMOUTH STEAM RAILWAY

Queens Park Station, Torbay Road, Paignton, Devon ☎ 0364 42338

7 miles

19

SEVERN VALLEY RAILWAY

Bewdley Station, Bewdley, Worcestershire DY12 1BE ☎ 0299 403816

16 miles

20

STRATHSPEY RAILWAY

The Railway Station, Boat of Garten, Inverness ☎ 047983 692

5 miles **

21

SWANAGE RAILWAY

Swanage Station, Swanage, Dorset BH19 1HB ☎ 0929 425800

3 miles *

22

WEST SOMERSET RAILWAY

Minehead Station, Minehead, Somerset TA24 5BG ☎ 0643 4996

20 miles

23

YORKSHIRE DALES RAILWAY

Embsay Station, Skipton, North Yorkshire BD23 6AX ☎ 0756 4727

2 miles **

NARROW GAUGE

† Narrow-gauge lines built on old standard-gauge trackbed by present-day enthusiasts.

‡ Not exactly 'preserved', these are minimum gauge (15-inch) and 12-inch gauge lines built specifically as tourist railways.

24

BALA LAKE RAILWAY

Llanuwchllyn Station, Bala, Gwynedd LL23 7DD ☏ 0678 4666

$4\frac{1}{2}$ miles †

25

BRECON MOUNTAIN RAILWAY

Pant Station, Merthyr Tydfil, Mid Glamorgan ☏ 0685 4854

2 miles †

26

FAIRBOURNE AND BARMOUTH STEAM RAILWAY

Beach Road, Fairbourne, Dolgellau, Gwynedd ☏ 0341 250362

$2\frac{3}{4}$ miles ‡

27

FESTINIOG RAILWAY

Harbour Station, Porthmadog, Gwynedd ☏ 0766 2384

$13\frac{1}{2}$ miles

28

ISLE OF MAN RAILWAY

Terminus Building, Strathallan Crescent, Douglas, Isle of Man ☏ 0624 74549

$15\frac{1}{4}$ miles

29

LAUNCESTON STEAM RAILWAY

Launceston, Cornwall ☏ 0566 5665

2 miles †

30

LEIGHTON BUZZARD NARROW GAUGE RAILWAY

Page's Park Station, Billington Road, Leighton Buzzard, Bedfordshire

☏ 0525 373888

$2\frac{3}{4}$ miles

31

RAVENGLASS & ESKDALE RAILWAY

The Station, Ravenglass, Cumbria ☎ 06577 226

7 miles ‡

32

ROMNEY, HYTHE AND DYMCHURCH RAILWAY

New Romney Station, Kent TN28 8PL ☎ 0679 62353

13¾ miles ‡

33

SITTINGBOURNE AND KEMSLEY LIGHT RAILWAY

The Walk, Milton Regis, Sittingbourne, Kent ME10 3HJ ☎ 0795 24899

2 miles

34

SNOWDON MOUNTAIN RAILWAY

Llanberis, Gwynedd LL55 4TY ☎ 0286 870223

4¾ miles

35

TALYLLYN RAILWAY

Wharf Station, Tywyn, Gwynedd LL36 9EY ☎ 0654 710472

7½ miles

36

VALE OF RHEIDOL RAILWAY

The Station, Aberystwyth, Dyfed ☎ 0970 612377

11½ miles

37

WELSHPOOL AND LLANFAIR LIGHT RAILWAY

The Station, Llanfair Caereinion, Powys SY21 0SF ☎ 0938 810441

8 miles

STEAM CENTRES

38

BIRMINGHAM RAILWAY MUSEUM

670 Warwick Road, Tyseley, Birmingham B11 2HL ☎ 021 7074696

39

BRESSINGHAM LIVE STEAM MUSEUM
Bressingham Hall, Diss, Norfolk IP22 2AB ☎ 037988 386

40

BUCKINGHAMSHIRE RAILWAY CENTRE
Quainton Road Station, Aylesbury, Buckinghamshire HP22 4BY ☎ 029675 450

41

DIDCOT RAILWAY CENTRE
Didcot Station, Didcot, Oxfordshire ☎ 0235 817200

42

NATIONAL RAILWAY MUSEUM
Leeman Road, York ☎ 0904 21261

43

STEAMTOWN RAILWAY CENTRE
Warton Road, Carnforth, Lancashire ☎ 0524 732100

PICTURE ACKNOWLEDGEMENTS

Page numbers in italics indicate colour photographs

JOHN ASHMAN HON. FRPS page 61; BBC HULTON PICTURE LIBRARY page 141; BRITISH RAIL page 16; DEREK CROSS pages *92–93, 94 (bottom left), 129, 130, 131 (top and centre), 132 (top), 133 (bottom)*; BRIAN DICKSON page 115; MIKE ESAU pages 26, 37, 147, 149, 160; FESTINIOG RAILWAY page 157; GREAT CENTRAL RAILWAY page 151; IAN KRAUSE page 142; NICK LERA pages 12, *134 (top), 135 (top)*; NORMAN LOCKETT pages *89, 90, 91, 95 (centre and bottom), 132 (bottom), 133 (top and centre)*; R C RILEY pages 46, *94 (top and bottom right), 95 (top), 96, 131 (bottom), 134 (bottom), 135 (centre and bottom), 136,* 138 (top), 140, 143 (bottom), 159; DAVID WILCOCK pages viii, 13, 24, 25; D C WILLIAMS page 121; M R YORK page 18.

All other photographs were supplied by Ivo Peters.